GW01066150

Contract Administration *in the* Public Sector

SECOND EDITION, REVISED 2011

Elisabeth Wright, Ph.D., CPCM
and
William D. Davison, CPPO

Prepared for NIGP: The Institute for Public Procurement.
All rights are conveyed to NIGP upon completion of this book.

Contract Administration in the Public Sector, 2nd Edition

Information in this book is accurate as of the time of publication and consistent with generally accepted public purchasing principles. However, as research and practice advance, standards may change. For this reason, it is recommended that readers evaluate the applicability of any recommendation in light of particular situations and changing standards.

National Institute of Governmental Purchasing, Inc. (NIGP)
151 Spring Street
Herndon, VA 20170
Phone: 703-736-8900; 800-367-6447
Fax: 703-736-9639 Email: education@nigp.org

This book is available at a special discount when ordered in bulk quantities. For information, contact NIGP at 800-367-6447. A complete catalog of titles is available on the NIGP website at www.nigp.org.

ISBN 1-932315-21-7
ISBN 978-1-932315-21-9

This book was set in Berkeley Oldstyle
Design & production by Vizuāl, Inc. - www.vizual.com.
Printed & bound by HBP.

Acknowledgements

The author wishes to acknowledge NIGP for its commitment toward advancing the theories and practices in procurement and contracting. Without their support this text would not have been possible.

Thanks and best,

Elisabeth Wright, Ph.D., CPCM
Program Manager
University of Mary Washington

I would like to acknowledge NIGP for their commitment to developing these textbooks which embrace the body of knowledge issued by the UPPCC based on theory and best practices and for NIGP's support and encouragement.

I am indebted to all of the procurement colleagues that I have had the privilege to work and learn with, who have shared their knowledge and experiences.

Mr. Bill D. Davison, CPPO
Purchasing Director
County of Stearns

Contents

Part I: Contract Administration

Chapter 1

Introduction

Scope

The management and administration of public sector contracts poses unique challenges. Billions of tax dollars are spent each year purchasing construction, supplies, and services in support of public facilities and services. The unique features of public sector contracts and the special obligations that accompany the expenditure of public funds complicate contract management.

The focus of contract administration is the achievement of stated goals and objectives through contract performance. The field embraces a longstanding recognition of three broad goals: a quality product, on time, and within budget. To achieve such goals, thoughtful contract administration must take a two-pronged approach: process and product focus. However, the extent of emphasis on process will vary, depending on the specifics of the contractual arrangement.

Many pitfalls and problems linger along the contract administration road. The contract manager must understand the complexities of the contracting environment and the dynamics that shape and influence the contracting process. Effective contract administration is difficult. The pre-award and award states of contract management form the framework for the contract administration phase. However, it is during the contract administration phase that the contract manager, along with a designated Contract Administration Team, must successfully stay the course, or alter the course, as circumstances may dictate.

Contract administration must be practiced with full attention to applicable laws, regulations, and policies. As important, the contract manager must exercise good judgment and apply critical thinking to the contract decisions that must be made. The contract manager's knowledge and the ability to apply reasoning and analytical skills to the decision-making process are critical components of successful contract administration.

This book provides a framework for examining contract administration by focusing on essential elements of the discipline. It also provides the reader with a focused look at key considerations related to important contract terms and conditions that must be enforced during contract administration. The intent is for the reader to develop a strong understanding of the complexities of contract administration and recognize the importance of planning, monitoring, and proactive insight into and oversight of contract performance.

Content

The scope of this work is limited. To address in sufficient detail all aspects of contract administration that could possibly affect all contracts would require an extensive work, such as an encyclopedia. Rather, the text has been designed to provide an understanding of the common contract administration functions that must be successfully performed and the implications associated with them. The topics addressed span the key contract administration functions that require specific attention during contract performance. Examples are offered as a means of further amplifying points within selected topical areas.

Additionally, this book offers best practices that have been adopted in the field. The reader is cautioned that while the fundamentals of good contract administration generally remain unchanged, the tools and techniques for effective administration evolve due to the dynamics of the internal and external operating environments. Most important, "one size does not fit all." The relationship between the contracting parties, the risk and the stated outputs and outcomes of each contract shape the methodology that will effect good contract administration.

Public organizations utilize various policies, regulations, and statutes to effect procurement. The Model Procurement Code is used by some procurement organizations, while others use a more streamlined procedure found in the Model Procurement Ordinance. At the central or Federal Government level, there is typically a common framework for procurement activities, e.g., the Federal Acquisition Regulations (FAR) promulgated by the U.S. Federal Government. Regardless of the regulatory or policy-driven framework that governs an organization's procurement and contracting operations, the concepts and their application are well recognized and used. Additionally, it is important to remember that the framework is simply that, and the good business judgment and use of sound analytical skills can influence good procurement decisions.

Organization

This book addresses the major areas of public contracting. It contains an overview of major topical areas that is augmented by an in-depth discussion of special interest areas and is divided into four parts:

Part I: Introduction to Contract Administration

Part II: The Planning and Implementation Phase

Part III: Contract Administration: Concepts and Application

Part IV: Contract Closeout Activities

Part I provides a general overview of contract management and contract administration.

Part II discusses the planning phase through the formation of the contract, which ideally begins with the development of solicitation documents. It then reviews the various planning techniques that allow for performance monitoring. A single chapter addresses the value, roles, responsibilities, and ethical expectations of the Contract Administration Team. Finally, the text explores the post-award activities that should be initiated shortly after contract execution.

Part III provides a focused examination of concepts and key functions during the contract administration period. Inspection and acceptance, modifications, data deliverables, delays, dispute resolution and appeals, and contract payment issues are discussed in individual chapters. Special interest topics, such as Request for Equitable Adjustment (REA) and Alternative Dispute Resolution (ADR), are also examined.

Part IV addresses contract termination and contract closeout issues.

The material is organized so that any topic of interest can be reviewed by itself. Readers may choose to begin with the broad discussion of contract administration and continue through the special topics addressed in Part III. The table of contents serves as the index of the material contained in the book, and a list of recommended readings at the end of the text will assist readers in their search for more knowledge on a particular subject.

Intended Audience

This text is intended for all contract managers from entry level to those with significant experience, because it examines contract administration in the context of 21st Century contract challenges. The material is addressed from a global perspective, i.e., unique statutes and/or regulations may be mentioned. However, the material transcends state or national level interest by offering a look at the process and best practices that have application, regardless of unique laws and regulations that may govern.

Members of the Contract Administration Team will find particular topics of interest. For example, the discussion of Contract Administration Plans and surveillance techniques will benefit those responsible for technical monitoring and oversight of contractor performance.

Chapter 2

Defining the Parameters and Value of
Contract Management and Contract Administration

An Overview

The written contract represents the legal agreement between the parties. The terms and conditions, prices, and technical and/or performance requirements are contained within the contract. Agreements outside of the contract are generally not enforceable. Once the parties have executed the contract, the challenges of contract administration begin. The dynamics of the internal and external operating environments can have a significant impact on the contract administration phase and can make fulfillment of the responsibilities and obligations of the contract parties difficult. Nonetheless, the contract administration phase requires a thoughtful application and enforcement of the terms of the contract. Fortunately, the public procurement process recognizes the dynamics of the operating environment and provides for modifications to the contract, as the parties deem necessary and appropriate.

By defining the parameters and value of contract administration, this chapter will:

- Provide a historical perspective of contracting
- Identify the differences between contract management and contract administration
- Discuss the role of contract formation as a preamble to contract administration
- Compare differences between commercial (known as private) and public contract administration
- Examine the operating environment, evolving nature, purpose, and strategic contributions of contract administration as a tool that can be used as a means to an end.

Historical Perspective

Within the United States, the framework for public sector contracting has remained essentially unchanged despite ongoing changes in the national and international environments. Contracting as a societal function dates back to the Phoenicians. The Purchasing Department can be traced back to the 13th Century B.C. According to Professor Emeritus Harry Page at The George Washington University:

> Inscribed clay tablets from the 13th Century B.C. days of the Phoenician traders refer to persons serving as the Purchasing Department agents. The Holy Bible, in the Book of Deuteronomy, provides instructions for buyers in the honest use of weights and measures. Ancient purchase orders, written on parchment scrolls in the days of Julius Caesar, call for delivery of amphorae of wine, honey and oil (Page 1954).

Problems associated with procurement are not new. In 1915, H. B. Twyford offered the following insight:

> A Procurement Department staff which is entirely unsympathetic with the particular needs of the users of the material will fail to grasp what is one of the most essential things for their department. They will be dealing with papers and accounts instead of men and things (Twyford 1915).

In the United States, contracting has its roots in the purchases to support the Revolutionary War. Congressional records delineate the specific contracting authorities extended to the first quartermaster of the United States Army, John Milfin. Contractual authority was provided to the extent that purchases were necessary to support the operations of the revolutionary troops. As the nation grew and additional Cabinet-level agencies were created, authority to obligate funds in order to secure the services of commercial firms was extended. The state-level delegation to the procurement department followed. The goals of the contracting system have remained constant, despite fluctuations in importance: quality goods and services delivered on time at a reasonable price. Throughout the history of contracting in the United States, a recurring theme that focused (albeit at varying degrees of interest) on accountability and wise expenditure of tax dollars is consistent today.

Contract Management

Overview

The broad goals of contract management are to successfully complete the procurement of a particular good or service by assuring that the public sector receives the required services or goods on time, in the right quantity, of the right quality, and that the contractor is properly compensated. Achievement of these goals requires both parties to agree to perform according to specific obligations. To ensure that both parties fulfill their obligations, the parties should form a contract. After the contract is signed, both parties should refer to the contract for direction on how to handle foreseen and unforeseen issues, conditions, and problems that arise during the course of contract performance.

Excellence in contract management begins with the process of establishing contract goals, identifying potential difficulties, and then using procurement tools in the contract formation process to develop specifications and a contract that effectively addresses the established contract objectives. To paraphrase Dr. Steven Covey's philosophy, keep the end in mind at the beginning (Covey, 1990).

The time spent during contract formation will reduce the amount of time spent administrating contracts.

The establishment of contractual goals begins with identifying the typical contract risks and contract administration problems associated with different types of purchases. The next steps are to assess the level of the risk by determining the potential for occurrence each of the problems has for a specific type of purchase, and then to develop specifications, contract clauses, and a Contract Administration Plan (CAP) to address the potential problems. If contract goals are not established, the public sector may be in a position of having to react to events that occur during the course of contract performance. If contractual disputes occur and adequate contract language does not exist, contract administration will be difficult.

It is important that the procurement department play a hands-on role in the entire contract formation process. During this process, the procurement department can assist in developing specific contract goals and provide the internal customer (also referred to as end-user) with contract formation tools, such as specifications, price and delivery types, and general types of contracts that contain contract clauses designed to address the typical contract risks. This assistance will aid in the development of a plan for monitoring contract performance. The time spent during contract formation will reduce the amount of time spent administrating contracts.

Unfortunately, contract management is often neglected. A written or boilerplate contract is issued without regard to the specific requirements of the purchase. The consequences to the public sector for poor contract management are:

- end-user frustration because of poor contractor performance, especially in the area of timeliness and quality
- end-user less willing to try a different vendor
- lack of contractor accountability
- agency acceptance of poor quality
- increased costs
- under/overpayment to a contractor.

Contrasting Terms

The term "contract management" is often used to describe the contract administration phase; however, caution must be exercised so that the terms are not confused. The taxonomy should be understood. Although some may use the terms interchangeably, contract management is commonly used to describe the entire contracting process, from pre-solicitation activities through contract closeout. In short, contract management can be seen as a sequential cycle as demonstrated in Figure 1, consisting of two main components—contract formation and contract administration. The key components of this sequential cycle will serve as the framework for this text.

Contract Formation	Contract Administration
I. Specify Need Bid (Specs) • Performance • Design • RFP (SOW) **II. Identify Contract Risks and Establish Contract Goals to Manage Risk** • Proposal Risk • Surety/Liability Risk • Schedule Risk • Contractual Risk • Performance Risk • Price Risk **III. Select General Contract Type and Clauses** **General Contract Types** Supplies (definite and indefinite delivery) Capital outlay Professional Services Contracted Services Software Leases Small orders Construction **General contract clauses** General clauses (protect legal and financial interests) • Compliance with applicable laws • Insurance and bonds • Independent contractor • Indemnity • Force majeure (Act of God) • Non appropriation of funds • Data privacy, non discrimination, EEO Specific clauses (appropriate to a specific purchase) • Both parties' responsibilities • Inspection/rejection • Change order procedure • Key Personnel • Breach/Termination procedure • Dispute Resolution • Warranties • Acceptance • Payment	**IV. Performance Monitoring** • Define and designate contract administration team member roles. • Contract Orientation • Development of contract administration plan • Output monitoring/Outcome monitoring • Auditing contract performance • Inspection • Change Orders, when to and when not to issue Options for dealing with: • Delays • Disputes • Poor performance Breach procedures Termination procedures Alternatives to termination Final Acceptance Payment plans Contract Closeout **V. Analysis** After completion of contract review process with the Contractor and end-user to determine what went right and what went wrong. Incorporate results into next contract management cycle.

Figure 1. The Contact Management Cycle.

Contract Formation

C ontract formation is a series of pre-award procurement activities between an agency and a contractor that result in a contract. The procurement department offers value to the contract formation process by providing a set of procurement tools which aid in assessing the different risks for each type of purchase and establishing specific contractual goals to manage risk. Contract formation includes identifying contract risks, establishing contract goals to manage risk, and pre-award procurement activities that result in the development of a contract. In essence, the contract formation activities serve as a preamble to the administrative activities that will follow once the contract is executed.

Contract Administration

Definition

"Contract administration" is a term used to describe the functions that are performed after the parties have signed the contract (Sherman, 1996). As a precise term, contract administration refers to those activities that take place after contract award and can encompass a plethora of activities ranging from routine to unusual. Typical contract administration activities are goal oriented, aimed at ensuring enforcement of the contract terms and conditions while giving attention to the achievement of the stated output and outcome of the contract. In other words, contract administration is about much more than simply the enforcement of the contract language. It requires the contract manager to remain focused on the program goals and objectives. Good contract administration fails when program goals and objectives are not met. Contract administration includes the development of a Contract Administration Plan (CAP), performance monitoring, contract closeout, and analysis.

Contract administration activities include payment, monitoring of progress, inspection and acceptance, quality assurance, monitoring and surveillance, modifications, negotiations, contract closeout, and many others. The extent of performance of these activities will vary given the size, scope, and complexity of the contract and the terms and conditions that apply. One should not be lured into thinking that routine contract administration activities pose no challenges. Even the most routine activities can cause difficulties that must be managed during the administration phase. Thus, contract administration must be accomplished in a proactive rather than reactive manner. In this sense, contract administration should not evolve into crises management. A well designed Contract Administration Plan serves as an effective tool with which to frame the activities that must take place during contract administration. CAPs will be discussed in further detail in subsequent chapters.

Purpose

Contract administration must focus on achievement of stated goals and objectives that fall within the framework of the negotiated contract. Contract administration protects the rights of the parties and ensures that the obligations of the parties are met. From the public sector perspective, contract administration concerns itself with the wise expenditure of public funds and the design and application of a decision-making process, which results in outcomes that are in the best interests of the citizens it serves.

Comparison: Private and Public Contract Administration

The common goal of the contracting parties is the successful achievement of the stated goals and objectives of the program as contained within the contract. Notwithstanding this common goal, the parties to the contract have competing and conflicting interests. The parties to the contract should also share the common goal of program success. The rights and obligations of the parties differ significantly in commercial and public procurement. The recent movement toward a strategic procurement department model is to remind the contracting parties of the long-term benefits to be had when both parties work toward a common goal.

Commercial contracting parties are concerned with profitability. The profit motives that the parties share in commercial agreement account for the significant difference between commercial and government contracting. While public contract managers, as public servants, have a fiduciary duty of care and trust, the organizations they represent lack the profit motive. This provides the parties to the public sector contract with competing and conflicting goals. The profit motive is recognized as a legitimate motive.

Contracts in either environment consist of the elements listed in Figure 2 below. Note that the existence of some elements is mandated in public contracting and is optional in commercial contracts.

Element	Public/Government Contract Requirement	Private/Commercial Contract Requirement
Offer	Yes	Yes
Acceptance	Yes	Yes
Legal Purpose	Yes	Yes
Capacity	Yes	Yes
Consideration	Yes	Yes
In Writing	Yes	Sometimes
Signature	Yes	Sometimes

Figure 2. Comparing Requirements Based on Contract Elements.

The Uniform Commercial Code (UCC), which generally governs commercial contracting, has been adopted by all states in the United States. Since contract law is complicated and most terms are implied (i.e., not stated expressly), the UCC provides the framework and details the procedures for forming sales contracts. Many of the terms are implied in the contract. Additionally, the statute of frauds requires that commercial contracts valued in excess of $5,000.00 be in writing.

The Operating Environment

The dynamics of the operating environment pose unique challenges to the contract manager during the contract administration phase. Political, social, economic, and other factors shape and influence the contracting process. Given these dynamics, the framework for effective contract administration should be structured to recognize that changes may be necessary to meet the evolving needs and/or goals and objectives of the government. Effective contract administration requires situational awareness. Consider the challenges posed by environmental mandates. Changing legislative initiatives may require changes to existing contracts in order to ensure compliance by contractors with newly enacted environmental statutes. Political agendas can alter the stated outcomes of contracts and, in some cases, can obviate the need for the contract. For example, the perceived need to construct a new government facility may change with a new political administration. If a contract has been awarded for construction of the facility, contract termination may be necessary.

Technological advancements pose unique challenges for contract administration. The need to quickly proceed through the pre-award phase to secure information technology items can result in contract administration problems. Additionally, the speed with which changes in technology occur further complicates contract administration. Thus, technology refreshment clauses can serve as a protection within the contract to ensure that the requirements of the user are met. A common complaint proffered by many of the requirements managers is that the contracting process takes so long—that by the time the contract is awarded, the technology is obsolete.

Changes in the operating environment can impact availability of funding, e.g., the establishment of the Office of Homeland Security. Operating funds for the establishment and initial fiscal year operating budget for this office came from the existing budgets in place for established programs. A 10% across-the-board reduction in the operating budgets of existing programs was mandated to fund the operation of Homeland Security. Funding reductions such as these often wreak havoc on existing contracts. Such are the challenges that contract managers face in effecting good contract administration.

Evolving Nature and Purpose

While contracting has long been recognized as a necessary function within public and private organizations, its contribution to the overall effectiveness of the organizations has frequently gone unrecognized. Contracting, along with other administrative functions, was commonly viewed as a "backroom" process that was difficult to quantify in terms of contributions to organizational success.

Today, the pendulum has swung and contracting is recognized by many organizations as a critical component of their operations. In fact, significant attention has been given to opportunities intended to streamline contracting operations. Contracting functions are generally categorized into two broad groups: strategic and non-strategic. The non-strategic contractual requirements contribute to the ongoing support of the routine operations and maintenance of the organizations. Strategic contracting, on the other hand, supports the mission of the organization. Recent initiatives seek to examine strategic objectives of the procurement department, using a top-down approach, giving significant weight to analyses of the spending patterns of organizations. Rationalizing the supplier base and leveraging buying power are viewed as strategic objectives aimed at reducing administrative costs and the costs of goods and services acquired under contract. Neither quality nor schedule is sacrificed.

...the goal of contracting organizations... has remained virtually constant: on-time delivery of quality goods within the stated budget or agreed-to price.

Whether a pendulum shift or a paradigm change, there is a perceived movement away from a totally decentralized procurement function and towards a more centralized procurement department model. The coordination of the purchasing function through a central office or department offers economies of scale. Quantities can be used as leverage toward achieving better prices. Regardless of the approach adopted, the goal of contracting organizations (in particular, public contracting organizations) has remained virtually constant: on-time delivery of quality goods within the stated budget or agreed-to price.

Contracting for services also poses particular problems because, unlike products and supplies, services are not tangible; thus, difficulties associated with establishing appropriate measures of acceptable performance exist. Additionally, unlike supplies, services cannot be returned.

Strategic Contribution

Contract administration requires the effective and efficient management of executed contractual agreements. Contracts are created to meet validated requirements of public organizations. As a result, each contract makes some contribution to the operational effectiveness of any organization. As mentioned earlier in this chapter, strategic contracting describes contractual arrangements that are mission-oriented, i.e., contribute to the success of the mission of the organization. Non-strategic contracts support the routine, non-strategic requirements of an organization. For example, contractual arrangements of the Virginia Department of Transportation (VDOT) to solve highway problems by building new highways (such as the well known "mixing bowl" in Northern Virginia) represent efforts that make a strategic contribution to the mission of VDOT. Contracts that provide routine office supplies in support of VDOT efforts are non-strategic in nature.

Regardless of the level of contribution that any one contract makes to an organization, each remains important, for failure to meet the non-strategic goals of any organization can have serious consequences.

A Tool: A Means to an End

The contract is simply a tool, but it must be an effective tool. The success of any contract is measured by the success of the program that the contract supports. This is an important concept, for the contract manager who focuses purely on enforcement of the contract without appreciating program objectives will not succeed. The contract must be well constructed and thought out, and the contract manager must understand how to use the contract effectively during performance. Training, experience, and education are three means by which the contract manager can become better equipped to use the "contracting tool."

References

Covey, S. (1990). *The 7 habits of highly successful people.* New York, NY: Simon and Schuster.

Page, H. (1954). *History of Procurement.* Unpublished manuscript, George Washington University.

Sherman, S. N. (1996). *Government Procurement Management.* Germantown, MD: Wordcrafters Publications.

Twyford, H.B. (1915). *Purchasing; its economic aspects and proper methods.* New York: D. Van Nostrand Company, Inc.

Part II: The Planning & Implementation Phases of Contract Administration

Chapter 3

Considerations for Affecting Contract Administration during the Formation Period

B efore beginning to consider the actual activities involved in contract administration, it is prudent to look at the aspects of contract formation that can have a particularly significant influence on contract administration. During the planning stage of the procurement process, much of the groundwork for contract administration is established. It is at this time that the end-user and contracting personnel should reach agreement in several important areas that impact contract administration. The specific pre-award activities that occur during the contract formation process are:

- identifying contract risks and establishing goals to manage risk
- determining the appropriate mechanism for developing a bid or proposal
- determining the appropriate type of contract.

Identifying Contract Risks and Establishing Contract Goals to Manage Risk

W hen identifying contract risks, it is important to remember that the contract will be read and interpreted by an array of people who represent a variety of special interests, and who read it for different reasons. A key goal during contract formation, therefore, is to eliminate the possibility of differing interpretations of the intent of the contract.

There are a number of possible problems that can result from either party misinterpreting contract requirements, including unsatisfactory performance, delays in delivery, and disputes over the obligations of both parties. There can be a lot at stake in addressing these types of problems. For example, if there is serious disagreement as to what is required under the terms of a contract and the contractor's work is called into question, there will be a need to establish responsibility. The public agency wants to avoid a situation where the contractor is misled or where ambiguous language leads to multiple interpretations.

With this understanding, it is important to note that each category of purchase, previously identified in this chapter, has risks associated with it. As noted in Figure 3, different types of purchases have different risks. By remaining involved in all pre-award activities, the procurement department can establish contract goals to effectively manage the risk. The Procurement Department must ask the end-users what is important to them. Procurement professionals can then develop appropriate contract clauses to anticipate any problems, manage the risk, and protect the agency's interests. This will assist in the contract administration process.

Purchase Category	Types of Contract Risks						
			Contractural				
	Proposal	Surety/Liability	Changes	Disputes	Breach/Termination	Schedule	Performance	Price
Small Orders Finite Delivery	X					X		
Term Orders Infinite Delivery	X				X	X		
Capital Outlay	X					X	X	X
Professional Services (Architects)	X	X	X	X			X	X
Contracted Services (Custodial)	X	X		X	X		X	
Software	X	X	X	X	X	X	X	X
Leases	X	X		X		X		X
Construction	X	X	X	X	X		X	X

Figure 3. Comparison of Contract Risks and Purchase Types.

Abi-Karam (2001) suggests that every purchase should be evaluated for six types of risks:

- *Proposal Risk*: Describes the item or service purchased through specifications and legal document(s)
- *Surety/Liability Risk*: Protects the financial and legal interests of the agency
- *Contractual Risk*: Establishes change/amendment procedures, dispute resolution, and breach procedures
- *Schedule Risk*: Ensures timely delivery

- *Performance Risk*: Defines acceptance

- *Price Risk*: Defines payment terms.

Several of these types of risks are addressed in separate chapters of this text; however, an overview of each type is provided below.

Proposal Risk: The Legal Document of Purchase

The contract is the document that the courts will refer to in the event of any legal disputes. The adage of "if it's not in writing, it doesn't exist" generally will hold true. The sources of public contract law are: federal, state and local statutes, general contract law (Uniform Commercial Code), and common law (a collection of court decisions regarding procurement). The contract language must be clear and concise. Avoid using ambiguous phrases that may lead to contract disputes if the contractor and the public agency cannot agree on their meaning. When a phrase is ambiguous, the intent of the contract will generally be interpreted in favor of the party that did not write the contract—usually the contractor. Examples of ambiguous phrases to avoid include the following (adapted from Harney, 1992):

- accurate workmanship
- as directed by
- best commercial practices
- clean and orderly
- highest grade and quality
- of a standard type
- to be furnished, if requested
- unless otherwise directed
- as determined by
- as soon as possible
- carefully performed
- good working order
- in the judgment of
- of an approved type
- to the satisfaction of
- workmanlike manner
- in accordance with applicable published specifications and industry standards

According to *The Contract Cookbook for Purchase of Services* (Short, 1987), if the contract document is printed, any typewritten changes will prevail. However, any handwritten entry on a typewritten document will prevail over typewritten terms. A quantity written out in words prevails over that expressed in numbers, if they differ.

Case law places a great weight on anything written in a "conspicuous" manner, i.e., larger font or contrasting type or color. Case law also establishes that the courts will always seek to find a legal and valid interpretation of a contract, unless the opposite is clearly established; but the courts usually feel that the person(s) drafting the contract fully understands the document. As a result, the courts interpret such documents more favorably for the party who did not draft the contract in those cases where the courts find two or more ways of interpreting the scope of the contract.

Surety and Liability Risks: Protection of Financial and Legal Interests

Protecting the financial and legal interests of the agency is an important contract goal. The contract should clearly define the following items:

- the mutual areas of agreement
- insurance requirements
- licensing
- indemnity
- equal employment opportunity

- a set of responsibilities for each party
- bonds
- data privacy
- nondiscrimination
- independent contractor

Contractual Risk: Establishing Change Order Procedures

The contract is a living document, and allowances must be made to accommodate unforeseen conditions that may affect the contract. The contract should specify who has the authority to make changes, how changes will be made in writing, and what changes will be unilateral.

The contract is a

living document...

to accommodate

unforeseen

conditions...

The contract should also specify how disputes will be resolved, if mutual agreement cannot be reached. Finally, the contract should also specify the breach notification process and the steps to cure a breach. This text provides detailed information on contract modifications, disputes, and terminations in separate chapters.

Schedule Risk: Ensuring Timely Delivery

The contract should contain clear and specific language describing the contract deliverables, delivery terms, and any penalties. This text provides detailed information on inspection and acceptance in a separate chapter.

Performance Risk: Defining Acceptance

The contract will define the conditions under which acceptance will occur and what type of inspection will be required. This text provides detailed information on defining acceptance in a separate chapter.

Price Risk: Defining Payment Terms

The contract will define how and when the contractor will be paid. The payment options include prepayment, progress payment, and final payment. It is important to link any payment terms to specific contract deliverables and a work plan. The public agency should only issue progress payments after specific delivery milestones are achieved and should only issue final payment after final acceptance occurs. This text provides detailed information on contract payment in a separate chapter.

Determining the Appropriate Mechanism for Developing a Bid or Proposal

When focusing on the product or service to be delivered to the public agency, there are four basic control mechanisms that can be implemented during the bid or proposal development phase that can significantly influence contract administration:

- effective contract specifications
- the type of contract pricing
- the acquisition method
- the type of delivery requirements

Writing Effective Contract Specifications

Contract administration problems can be created even before a contract is awarded. This is most likely to be the case when an organization is unsure of exactly what it wants to purchase or when the purchase is needed but the requirements are inadequately defined. The element of a contract that is most likely to create administrative problems is the statement of the requirement, which is variously referred to as the specification or the Statement of Work (SOW).

Effective contract performance depends on the contractor's ability to interpret the technical requirements that have been established. The SOW should reflect what is required and establish the procedure by which it will be determined that all requirements of the contract have been met. There are four basic approaches to stating contract requirements.

- *Design Specifications.* A design specification describes the specifics of the item, such as the size, dimensions, materials, physical requirements, quality tests, etc. A design specification gives a public agency more control over the item being delivered because the public agency determines what the contractor will provide. When it is critical for items to meet existing or predetermined specifications, the specification should be more rigid or detailed so that more control can be exerted over the contractor. However, the more detailed the specification, the responsibility the public agency has for ensuring that the detailed spe complete and accurate and that the quality of the item received durin is consistent with the specification. This also means that the public agency has a greater responsibility for eliminating errors, omissions, or deficiencies in the specification prior to its release in a bid or proposal. This action will impact the contract administration effort, especially in the areas of inspection and testing.

- *Performance Specifications.* A performance specification expresses the purchaser's desired performance characteristics in terms of output and function. A performance specification leaves the details of design to the contractor and states the overall performance need, allowing the contractor to furnish the item to meet that need. A performance specification gives the contractor more flexibility than a design specification in determining the design of an item, thereby allowing the contractor to use ingenuity in responding to the requirements. However, a performance specification also requires the contractor to accept greater responsibility for the design and achievement of the performance requirements stated in the contract. This will impact the contract administration effort, especially in the area of acceptance.

- *Combination Design and Performance Specifications.* Combination design and performance specifications incorporate, to the degree necessary, the attributes of both the performance and design specifications.

- *Statement of Work.* The Statement of Work (SOW) is a broad narrative that describes an agency's need and a desired outcome or level of work to be achieved. The contractor is responsible for developing a work plan to meet the agency goals.

Selecting the Acquisition Method

A second control mechanism that has an effect on contract administration is the method of acquisition. The Model Procurement Code, produced by the American Bar Association (ABA) in conjunction with sponsorships from other prominent associations like the National Institute of Governmental Purchasing (NIGP), identifies four methods of acquisition.

Small Purchase Procedures. Simplified procurement procedures are used to accommodate low dollar requirements. Simplified informal procedures may include sending no documentation other than terms (price, quantity, quality, and delivery) prior to the purchase of goods. This reduces procurement lead time and costs. Inspection and delivery monitoring is usually the only contract administration activity performed.

Competitive Sealed Bid (CSB). A competitive sealed bid is used for requirements exceeding the small purchase dollar limit and is the preferred method of source selection in accordance with the ABA's *2000 Model Procurement Code for State and Local Public Agencies*. When the contract is of a high dollar amount, documentation protecting the public agency's financial interest (bonds, insurance, detailed acceptance procedures) is included as part of the bid. The level of contract administration is dependent on the complexity of the purchase.

Request for Proposal (RFP). Professional services, software, and complex projects are typically purchased through this method. The critical component of an RFP is the SOW. The SOW lists the requisite requirements to attain the contract. For example, in the case of a desired service, the SOW should detail the particular problem to be solved. In most cases, the SOW outlines the outcomes but does not mandate the specific approach the contractor must take.

The RFP document contains detailed language describing acceptance and protection of the public agency's financial interests. The terms may be negotiable and are often an important part of the award process. The potential contractor who submits a proposal (often referred to as the "offeror") will often submit a work plan.

Contract administration can be complex due to the unique circumstances and terms surrounding the RFP process. It is important to include contract documents with the RFP so that the offeror is able to review all of the proposed contract terms and conditions. By submitting a response, the offeror agrees to the terms and conditions contained in the RFP document or may propose contract changes as terms for negotiation.

For Competitive Sealed Bids or Request for Proposal, there is the option of conducting a Pre-Bid/Pre-Proposal Conference. This conference provides the procurement department an opportunity to review the key elements of the contracts with potential contractors, such as delivery date, key personnel, quality and payment schedules, outcomes, and measurements. The potential contractors, in turn, have an opportunity to bring up any questions on these issues, thereby reducing future misunderstandings.

In the case of an RFP or for any type of acquisition where terms are negotiated, an offeror may respond to a solicitation by submitting proposed contract changes, or they may substitute their own standard contract. From a contract administrative perspective, it is critical for the procurement department to assess the following key provisions:

- Applicable Law: The offeror may select a different venue.
- Limitation of Liability: The offeror's proposed limit is lower than required.
- Termination: The clauses may conflict with specifications. The offeror may provide for termination for convenience with shorter notice than permitted by the public agency.
- Alternative Dispute Resolution: The offeror may require that arbitration be used. This procedure could deny the agency the right of a trial.
- Indemnification: The agency may be required to indemnify the offeror, pay attorney's fees, reimburse costs, and pay termination costs.
- Payment: The offeror may require advance payments prior to the delivery of goods or services.

Sole Source and Emergency Purchases. Many agencies require justification prior to using either the sole source or emergency process. Under these circumstances, the public agency would define parameters through an SOW, and the offeror would respond with a proposal. The actual acquisition function would depend on the public agency's regulations governing sole sources and emergencies. For emergency purchases, the main focus is on documenting what is purchased and where it is purchased.

Selecting the Type of Contract Pricing

A third pre-award control mechanism that has a significant impact on contract administration is determining what type of pricing is to be used for a contract. Different price types establish different relationships between a contractor and the public agency, thereby influencing the nature and the extent of contract monitoring to be performed. Figure 4 provides a guide to these major categories of contract pricing and their applicability and limitations.

	Applicability	Essential Elements	Limitations
Firm-Fixed Price	Fair and reasonable price can be established at inception, e.g. • Reasonably definite design or performance specifications • Realistic estimates • Adequate competition • Valid cost or operating data that provide reasonable price comparisons	Initial fixed-price places 100% responsibility and risk on contractor	Government and contractor must agree on fixed-price at inception
Fixed-Price with Escalation	Market or labor conditions unstable over extended production period	Ceiling on upward adjustment; downward adjustment appropriate where elements escalated may fall below base levels provided in contract	Contingencies are industry-wide and beyond contractor control; contingencies must be specifically defined in the contract
Fixed-Price Incentive	Where cost uncertainties exist and there is the possibility of cost reduction and/or perfor-mance improvements by giving contractor (i) a degree of cost responsibility and (ii) a positive profit incentive	Firm Target: target cost; target profit; price ceiling; and profit adjustment formula	Adequate contractor accounting system required. Must determine that any other contract type is impractical. Used for development and production procurement
	Firm Target Type: firm target and final profit adjustment formula can be negotiated initially		

	Applicability	Essential Elements	Limitations
Fixed-Price with Re-determination	Stated Time or Times: quantity production–, realistic price can be negotiated initially but not for later period(s) of performance	Stated Time or Times: fixed-price initially; prospective re-determination, upward or downward; a specific time or times for re-determination; price ceiling if appropriate	Adequate contractor accounting system required. Stated Time or Times: firm fixed-price not possible; length of pricing period, 12 months or more, reasonable assurance of prompt re-determination
	Retroactive After Completion: realistic fixed-price cannot be negotiated initially; amount so small or time so short	Retroactive After Completion: ceiling price; agreement to negotiate price after performance	Retroactive After Completion: research and development of $100,000 or less only fair and reasonable billing price
Cost and Cost-Sharing	Uncertainties in performance–Impossible to estimate costs firmly Cost: R&D with nonprofit organizations or educational institutions; facilities contract	Uncertainties in performance–Impossible to estimate costs firmly Cost: Government pays cost; no fee	
	Cost Sharing: development or research projects jointly sponsored by government and contractor where contractor anticipates commercial benefit in lieu of fee under the contract	Cost Sharing: Government pays agreed predetermined portion of costs; no fee	Adequate contractor accounting system required. Cost Sharing: must present evidence that there is high probability that contractor will receive substantial present or future commercial benefits
Cost-Plus-Incentive Fee	Uncertainties in performance–Impossible to estimate costs firmly. Development and test when incentive formula can provide positive incentive for effective management. Where feasible, use performance incentives together with cost and schedule incentives	Uncertainties in performance–Impossible to estimate costs firmly Target cost; target fee; minimum and maximum fee; fee adjustment formula (formula applied at end of performance)	Adequate contractor accounting system required Fee Limitations Production & Services-10% est. cost R&D-15% est. cost Formula should provide incentive effectiveness over variation in costs throughout the full range of reasonable foreseeable variation from target cost
Cost-Plus-Fixed-Fee	Uncertainties in performance–Impossible to estimate costs firmly. Term Form: research preliminary exploration, or study when level of effort is initially unknown (or development and test when a CPIF is impractical) Completion Form: research or other development effort when the task or job can be clearly defined, a definite goal or target expressed, and a specific end product required	Uncertainties in performance–Impossible to estimate costs firmly Negotiated estimate of costs; fee fixed initially except for changes in the work or services required	Adequate contractor accounting system required. Fee Limitations: Production & Services-10% est. cost R&D-15% est. cost Not for development of major weapons once exploration indicates engineering development is feasible

	Applicability	Essential Elements	Limitations
Time and Materials (Labor-Hours)	Not possible initially to estimate extent or duration of work (L-H used where materials not involved) e.g., engineering or design services; repair, main-tenance, or overhaul	Direct labor hours speci-fied at fixed hourly rates; direct materials at "cost." Ceiling price shall be established	Determination that no other type of contract is suitable
Letter Contract	Exigency requires immediate bind-ing agreement so work can begin but time does not permit negotia-tion of a definitive contract	Maximum government liability, type of definitive contract, as many defini-tive contract provisions as possible	No other contract type suitable

Figure 4. Comparison of Contract Risks and Purchase Types.

There are two major types of contract pricing: fixed price and cost reimbursement. There are also several variations to each type. The principal goal of contract administration is the same for both fixed-price and cost-reimbursement contracts: to ensure that the requirement is satisfied in a timely manner and at a reasonable cost. However, the specific concerns and related activities that comprise the administration function vary depending on the type of contract. Because of the significant differences in the two types of pricing contracts, it is important to use them appropriately.

Fixed-priced contracts are appropriate when it is possible to accurately predict the costs involved in accomplishing a contract assignment and when it is reasonable to ask the contractor to assume responsibility for all costs. Fixed-price contracts are generally used when an organization can clearly specify what it wants to buy and that there are no uncertainties anticipated during the performance of the assignment.

Cost-reimbursement contracts are used when there is uncertainty, a variety of unknown potential cost risks, and when it is unreasonable to ask a contractor to assume these risks alone.

In fixed-price contracts, the focus of contract administration is to ensure that the contractor complies with the specifications set forth in the contract. In cost-reimbursement contracts, the specification or SOW may be less definitive, and the focus of contract administration is largely concerned with establishing the precise methods and manner of performance as the work progresses.

In a fixed-price contract, the contractor is responsible for managing all costs, regardless of whether they exceed or fall below the total contract price. The contractor usually agrees to complete the work before being paid, though work can be broken down into stages of contract performance or, in the case of maintenance contracts, be paid in full at the beginning of the contract. The total amount of predetermined payment cannot be exceeded and reflects the end result of the contract effort.

On the other hand, in a cost-reimbursement contract, the contractor is reimbursed for all allowable costs incurred during performance. The contractor commits to making a best effort to complete all work. The total amount to be paid to the contractor is not fixed at the outset, but it is highly recommended that a ceiling cost be established. The initial ceiling cost can be increased by contract modification if circumstances warrant. Payment is for the contractor's effort and is paid upon incremental results of that endeavor.

...in a cost-reimbursement contract, the contractor is reimbursed for all allowable costs incurred during performance.

From the public agency's contract administration perspective, there is also a difference in the degree of responsibility for managing contract costs. For fixed-price contracts, the contractor accepts most, if not all, of the cost risk. The agency should not interfere in the way in which the project is managed. The contractor should be allowed to make major decisions regarding the use of resources and the control of the work. This means less contract administration and monitoring by the agency. In cost-reimbursement contracts, the public agency is assuming most, if not all, of the risk and responsibility and, therefore, has a keen interest in the use of resources and the way in which the work is proceeding. Staff should play a more active oversight role, which, in turn, means more contract administration responsibility.

Variations of Fixed-Priced Contracts

There are several types of fixed-price contracts, and the extent of administrative activity may vary. The following are the four most commonly used fixed-price types, with brief descriptions of their respective characteristics.

Firm Fixed Price. The firm fixed price contract is the most commonly used type of contract. Under this scenario, the contractor assumes full responsibility and risk for completing the project or purchase. The total cost is specified when the contract is awarded and is based on the initial specifications or SOW. There are no adjustments to price based on the contractor's performance. This type of pricing provides the greatest incentive for effective cost control because the contractor keeps any savings realized. Contract administration concerns focus on delivery and inspection.

Fixed Price with Escalation (Fixed Price with Economic Price Adjustment). A fixed price with escalation contract provides for upward or downward adjustment of price based on certain contingencies that are specified in the contract. This type of pricing is used when there is concern about the stability of the market and labor conditions during a period when production is to take place and when it is possible to identify contingencies. Pricing adjustments are made according to provisions included in the contract, providing a basis for price increase or decrease. (The basis is often a specific index of wage rates or raw materials costs.)

In this type of contract, the contractor and the public agency share the risks and potential benefits. The contractor is protected against unusual price increases, but the public agency will save money if costs decrease. If the contingencies specified in the contract do not occur, the contract is the equivalent of a firm-fixed-price contract. The primary performance risk is still on the contractor, and the contractor's profit will not change as a result of any cost increases or decreases. Contract administration concerns for this type of pricing include:

- Making sure that price changes are handled properly (in accordance with the contract provisions)

- Verifying the validity of all requests for increased compensation

- Making sure that the public agency receives the benefits of any price reductions.

Fixed-Price-Incentive. A fixed-price-incentive contract provides for the adjustment of profit and the establishment of a final price through the use of a formula that compares the total actual costs to initial target costs. This type of pricing is used when achievable cost and performance goals exist beyond the target or minimum acceptable levels established by the contract and achievement goals serve as profit incentives for the contractor. If final costs are above the target and/or performance is below the target, the contractor's profit is reduced. If final costs are below the target and/or performance is above the target, the contractor's profit is increased. Administrative tasks associated with this type of pricing include:

- A continual audit of the contractor's cost and measurement of its performance in order to apply the predetermined formula incentive

- Negotiating final agreements based on costs

- Establishment of firm rules of cost allowances and allocations

- Managing contract modifications that may result in the need to adjust the incentive part of the contract.

Fixed-price-incentive contracts can have both performance and cost incentives. If performance exceeds targeted standards, the contractor's profit will increase. If performance falls short of targeted standards, profit will decrease. Cost incentives are measured against established targets. Higher costs will reduce profit, while lower costs will increase profit. This type of performance-based contract is appropriate for contracted services for the purpose of rewarding high quality performance. An example is a custodial services contract in which performance goals are established, such as scoring "excellent" on 95% of the weekly customer inspection reports. If the contractor exceeds the goals, a predetermined "incentive" is paid.

Fixed Price with Re-determination. A fixed price with re-determination contract is used when a realistic price can be determined for initial periods but not for subsequent periods, e.g., a contract for the development of a prototype. The contractor has the cost risk for the initial determination and the public agency for the re-determination. Contract administrators must make sure that the initial goal is well defined and monitored.

Variations of Cost-Reimbursement Contracts

There are also a variety of cost-reimbursement-type contracts that are appropriate under any of the following circumstances:

- When the uncertainties of a contract effort cannot be estimated reasonably

- When a contractor's cost accounting system is adequate for accurately determining the exact costs that apply to that contract

- When an organization is confident that personnel assigned to monitor performance will be able to determine whether the contractor is using inefficient or wasteful methods.

Cost Plus Fixed Fee. In a cost-plus-fixed-fee contract, the contractor is reimbursed for all reasonable, allocable, and allowable costs. The contractor receives a fixed fee (profit) amount negotiated at the time of award. There are two types of cost-plus-fixed-fee contracts: completion form and term form. A completion form cost contract identifies a specific task or goal and specifies an end product. The contractor is normally required to complete and deliver the specified end product within the estimated cost. A term form cost contract commits the contractor to a specified level of effort based on the general SOW for a specified period of time.

Cost Plus Incentive Fee. A cost-plus-incentive-fee contract is used when a formula can provide an incentive for effective management. Targeted cost minimums/maximums and fee adjustment formulas are established at the outset. The contractor receives reimbursement for costs as in a cost-plus-fixed-fee contract, but the fee is determined after the contract is completed according to a formula comparing actual to targeted costs as in fixed-price-incentive contracts. Contract administration concerns include: (1) assessing how much of the possible incentive has been earned and (2) determining how contract modifications and changes in the requirements impact the incentive features.

Cost Sharing. A cost-sharing contract is used when it is impossible to estimate costs firmly and there is a high probability that the contractor will receive a substantial present or future commercial benefit. This type of contract may be used in research and development contracts, as well as public/private partnerships. The focus of contract administration is on monitoring performance and contractor costs and the privatization of utilities/landfills, roadways, etc.

Time and Materials. Time-and-materials contracts are used only when no other type of pricing is suitable. This type of pricing provides the contractor with a fixed rate for each hour of labor plus the cost of materials. (If no materials are involved, this is referred to as a "labor hour" contract.) A contract-ceiling price is negotiated at the outset of the contract. When this method of pricing is used, the contract administrators must closely monitor:

- the total labor hours charged to contract

- the progress of the work to ensure that time charged is productive

- the qualifications of employees assigned, especially because there is an economic incentive to the contractor to use fewer skilled workers than called for in the fixed labor rate.

Letter Contract. This type of contract allows for the work to begin before an agreement is reached on final contract terms and should be used only when it is necessary for the work to begin immediately and there is no time to negotiate the terms of a contract. This type of contract puts the public agency in a weaker position for negotiating favorable terms and prices. It is important that a contract is negotiated as soon as possible in order to protect the public agency's interests. The contract should establish limits as to how much work can be done, or how much time can pass, before the contract is agreed upon. Any changes in the SOW must be carefully considered, because the contract price has not yet been established.

Time-and-materials contracts are used only when no other type of pricing is suitable.

Selecting the type of Delivery Requirements

How and when the product or service is delivered is a fourth control mechanism that will affect the level of contract administration. There are two general types of delivery requirements and variations within these two major categories.

Definite Delivery. Definite delivery occurs when a specific requirement quantity and delivery date have been established. This is the most common type of delivery requirement. Common examples include one-time purchase orders and capital outlays. The focus of contract administration efforts is on monitoring the delivery schedule, inspection, and liquidated damages for delays.

Indefinite Delivery. Indefinite delivery contracts are suitable for commodity purchases because the products purchased are standard throughout the industry and there are numerous vendors. All of the indefinite delivery types of contracts should be used only with firm-fixed-price or fixed-price-with-escalation-pricing contracts. The focus of contract administration is on inspection for this type of agreement. There are three variations of indefinite delivery contracts:

- *Indefinite delivery with a definite quantity* occurs when a quantity of supplies or services is specified but the time of delivery is flexible. This type of delivery requirement is used where requirements are definite or have a short lead-time.

- *Indefinite quantity and indefinite delivery* contracts are used to establish a minimum and maximum quantity that can be ordered within a definite delivery period. This contract requirement is flexible in terms of both quantity and delivery schedule.

- *Requirement delivery contracts* are used when the public agency agrees to purchase all requirements for a certain period of time from the contractor. Under this scenario, the quantity of items and the number of deliveries is unspecified, thereby differentiating it from a definite type of contract, because specific quantities have not been established.

Determining the Appropriate Type of Contract

Categories of Goods and Services

Most of the goods and services purchased by a public agency fall into one of the following categories:

- small orders with a finite delivery quantity
- term orders with a finite or infinite delivery quantity
- capital outlay
- professional services (architects)
- contracted services (custodial services)
- software
- leases
- construction

With respect to these categories of purchases, the procurement department must anticipate the typical contract administration problems that may occur in each category of purchase by developing a general contract template for each category. The standardized commodity and/or service contract will address a majority of the contractual risks and typical contract administration problems associated with a particular type of purchase. After this template is developed, the specific clauses in the general contract should then be reviewed and removed or added, as needed, to meet specific contractual goals.

Typical Contract Administration Problems

During the contract administration process for any category of purchase problems may be encountered:

- wrong or unsatisfactory product is delivered
- delay in delivery or completion

- dispute over definition of acceptance (When will the project be completed?)
- change orders
- personality conflicts between the contractor and public agency representatives
- limited or no replacement sources of supply
- poor performance
- high risk of failure
- use of subcontractors
- high cost.

The cost of dealing with contract administration problems after they occur can be tremendous both in dollars and time. To effectively manage a contract, the procurement department should anticipate which contract administration problems are most likely be encountered and then develop specifications, contract clauses, and a contract-monitoring plan to avoid or manage the problems. According to research conducted by Davison and Sebastian the most likely contract administration problems to occur, for any type of contract, are delays and high costs (Figure 5). This research also found that Construction and Contracted Service contracts experience the greatest number of contract problems (Figure 5-1). A summary of the research findings is listed in Figure 5-2. For example for Construction contracts, change orders were perceived to be the most common problem encountered and other sources were the least likely problem to be encountered. With this information public procurement personnel can prepare specifications, contracts and contract administration plans to avoid or minimize the adverse impact of contract administration problems. Procurement personnel can effectively allocate scarce resources to the contracts or contract administration problems that are most likely to occur.

Contract Administration Problem	Mean	Rank
Delays	5.73a	1
Cost	6.13a	2
Change Order	6.16b	3
Poor Performance	6.36b	4
Definition of Acceptance	6.66c	5
Conflict	6.67cd	6
Other Sources	6.93d	7
Subcontractors	7.08de	8
Risk of Failure	7.24f	9
Wrong Product	7.29f	10

Figure 5. Perceived occurrence of contract administration problems over all types of contracts.

Note: Means that do not share a common subscript are significantly different at the .05 level.

ᵕvison, W. D., & Sebastian, R. J. (In press). The relationship between contract administration problems and ct type. Journal of Public Procurement. Reprinted with permission.

Contract Type	Mean	Rank
Construction	6.02a	1
Contracted Services	6.15a	2
Professional Services	6.23ab	3
Software	6.39b	4
Capital Outlay	6.67c	5
Supplies, Small Purchases	6.67c	6
Leases	6.72c	7

Figure 5.1. Perceived occurrence of contract administration problems by type of contract.

Note: Means that do not share a common subscript are significantly different at the .05 level.

Davison, W. D., & Sebastian, R. J. (In press). The relationship between contract administration problems and contract type. Journal of Public Procurement. Reprinted with permission.

Contract Type	Perceived Occurrence of Contract Administration Problems Ranking Order									
	1	2	3	4	5	6	7	8	9	10
Supplies and Small Purchases	Delays	Cost	Poor Performance	Change Order	Wrong Product	Other Sources	Conflict	Definition of Acceptanc	Risk of Failure or Termination	Sub contractor
Capital Outlay	Delays	Cost	Change Order	Poor Performance	Other Sources	Conflict	Sub contractor	Definition of Acceptance	Risk of Failure or Termination	Wrong Product
Professional Services	Change Order	Delays	Cost	Conflict	Definition of Acceptance	Poor Performance	Sub contractor	Other Sources	Risk of Failure or Termination	Wrong Product
Contracted Services	Risk of Failure or Termination	Definition of Acceptance	Change Order	Other Sources	Conflict	Cost	Sub contractor	Cost	Poor Performance	Delays
Software	Cost	Other Sources	Delays	Definition of Acceptance	Change Order	Poor Performance	Conflict	Risk of Failure or Terminatio	Wrong Product	Subcontractor
Leases	Cost	Other Sources	Delays	Poor Performance	Definition of Acceptance	Change Order	Conflict	Risk of Failure or Termination	Sub contractor	Wrong Product
Construction	Change Order	Delays	Cost	Subcontractor	Conflict	Definition of Acceptance	Poor Performance	Risk of Failure or Termination	Wrong Product	Other Sources

Figure 5.2 Perceived occurrence of contract administration problems for each contract type.

Davison, W. D., & Sebastian, R. J. (In press). The relationship between contract administration problems and contract type. Journal of Public Procurement. Reprinted with permission.

A Brief Look at Terms and Conditions

A standardized contract contains general and specific clauses designed to manage risk. The final step is to review all of the clauses in the contract's template and modify them, as necessary, to meet specific contract goals when developing a final contract.

The procurement department should review general or boilerplate clauses and reference current and applicable federal, state, or local laws. As an example, the insurance requirements may be different for a particular purchase. For architectural and other professional services, errors/omissions insurance may be required. Asbestos abatement projects may require high Workers' Compensation and liability insurance. Bonding requirements vary from project to project. Construction contracts may require insurance for materials stored on site and/or may require a bid bond, public construction, or payment and performance bond. For mission critical projects such as software, performance bonds are often a requirement.

Specific Contract Clauses

Specific contract clauses should be developed to address the contract administration problems. Figure 5-3 provides a good reference of typical contract administration problems that have been associated with each general contract type. Additional references and information for drafting a contract can be found in *The Legal Aspects of Public Purchasing, 2nd edition (Buffington & Flynn, 2008).*

General Contract Type	Wrong Product	Delays	Definition of Acceptance	Change Order	Conflict	Other Sources	Poor Performance	Risk of Failure/Terminate	Sub Contractors	Cost
Supplies and Small Purchases	X	X								
Capital Outlay	X	X						X		X
Professional Services (e.g. Architects)		X	X	X	X	X				
Contracted Services (e.g. Custodial)			X	X	X		X	X	X	
Software		X	X	X		X	X	X	X	
Leases				X	X	X	X			
Construction		X		X	X	X		X	X	X

3. Comparison of General Contract Types and Contract Administration Problems.

Supply and General Purchases

Inspection and Acceptance Clause. The less available a replacement, the more stringent the contract language should be regarding completion or delivery dates and possible delays. The higher the level of quality and the higher the cost of accepting a poor product, the stronger the inspection language must be.

Capital Outlay Purchases

Inspection and Acceptance Clause. The less available a replacement, the more stringent the contract language should be regarding delivery dates and delays. The higher the level of quality and the high cost of accepting a poor product, the stronger the inspection language must be.

...the contract could include a specific cost to be paid by the contractor, if delivery is delayed and additional costs are incurred...

Liquidated Damages. Depending on how critical the item or service is to the public agency's operation, the contract could include a specific cost to be paid by the contractor, if delivery is delayed and additional costs are incurred as a result of the delay. Consider the implications in delayed delivery of a snowplow. Because the snowplow needs to be ready prior to snowfall, if delivery is delayed, the contractor is responsible for the agency's cost of using a substitute until the correct product can be/is received.

Change Orders. The contract should define what unilateral changes are allowed and how change requests will be handled. Capital outlay purchases related to construction and software projects often encounter unforeseen circumstances.

Professional Services

Key Personnel. If a key person provided by the contractor is critical to the success of the project, there may be few qualified people to provide the specified services, if the contractor no longer employs this person.

Definition of Performance. Complex projects require specifically defined objectives and measurable outcomes related to performance.

Work Plan and Payment Plan. Specific deliverables in the work plan, such as meetings or reports must be achieved before making partial payment.

Change Orders. The contract should define what unilateral changes are allowed and how change requests will be handled. Professional service projects often encounter unforeseen circumstances.

Delays. How critical is this purchase to the public agency's operation? Usually, there is no other contractor qualified or available to complete the project, if the agency terminates the contract.

Dispute Resolution. How critical is it to keep the project moving forward? Can disputes be resolved through mediation or arbitration so that the project moves forward, even if a decision is rendered in the contractor's favor?

Contracted Services

Performance. How complex is the project and how much coordination is required within the agency? Has the level of effort been adequately defined so that both parties will know when an objective is achieved?

Dispute Resolution. How critical is it to keep the project moving forward? Can disputes be resolved through mediation or arbitration so that the project can move forward, even if a decision is rendered in favor of the contractor?

Termination. What are the criteria for terminating a contract? How expensive is it to start again? How easy is it to get another contractor?

Change Orders. How detailed are the specifications? Is the requested change already included in the project?

Subcontractor. How much control over other companies is necessary?

Software Acquisitions

Acceptance. How accurate are the goals that have been described? It is important to understand what is being purchased so it can be determined if the goal is met? Who is going to determine acceptance? The larger the numbers of people who have to agree on the purchase, the more difficult it is to reach consensus.

Dispute Resolution. How critical is it to keep the project moving forward? Can disputes be resolved through mediation or arbitration so that the project moves forward, even if a decision is rendered in favor of the contractor?

Delays. How critical is this purchase to the public agency's operation? Software is usually mission-critical, and delays are common. Is there a substitute product or vendor available? Software is usually unique to an agency. Similar packages exist, but can they be immediately substituted? Financial incentives are recommended.

Termination. What are the criteria for terminating the contract? How expensive is it to start again? How easy is it to secure another vendor? It is expensive to start over, so it is important to deliberate financial implications when considering termination.

Subcontractor. How much control over other companies is necessary?

Work Plan and Payment Plan. Can a specific deliverable in the work plan (i.e., meetings or reports) be linked to a partial payment? Is a customer acceptance test plan necessary?

Construction

Delays. How critical is this purchase to the public agency's operation? Construction delays are common. Is there a substitute product or vendor available? Financial incentives are recommended.

Subcontractor. How much control over other companies is necessary?

Performance Guarantees and Incentives. Usually, performance and payment bonds are required. Financial incentives for early completion linked with damage charges for late completion may be effective.

Work Plan and Payment Plan. Can a specific deliverable in the work plan, i.e., percentage of construction completed, be linked to partial payment?

References

Abi-Karam, T. (2001). *Managing risks in design/build, Technical programs and proceedings.* The Association for the Advancement of Cost Engineering (AACE) International, 45th Annual International Conference. Pittsburgh PA.

Buffington, K.W. & Flynn, M., Esq. (NIGP) (2007). The *legal aspects of public purchasing.* (2nd. ed.). Herndon, VA: NIGP.

Cibinic, J., Jr., & Nash, R. C., Jr. (1995). *Administration of Government Contracts* (3rd ed.). Washington, DC: The George Washington University.

Davison, W.D., & Sebastian, R.J. (2007). *Journal of Public Procurement.* The Relationship between Contract Administration Problems and Contract Type, by Permission. Boca Raton, FL.

Harney, D. (1992). *Service contracting—A Local Government Guide.* Washington, DC: International City/County Management Association (ICMA).

Short, J. (1987). *The Contract Cookbook for Purchase of Services.* Lexington, KY: The Council of State Public Agencies.

Thai, K.V., Ph.D. (2007). Introduction to public procurement. (2nd ed.). Herndon, VA: NIGP.

Chapter 4

Planning for Performance

An effective contract administration program will rely on pro-active planning documents that guide the public agency and the contractor towards exemplary performance. This chapter focuses on three planning tools to achieve performance outcomes.

- Contract Administration Plan and its components
- Performance Assessment Plan
- Surveillance techniques.

Contract Administration Plan (CAP)

There are three critical plans that are developed and utilized in various phases of the acquisition process:

- The Acquisition Plan, which sets the overarching strategy for the total acquisition process

- The Source Selection Plan, which details the source selection strategy

- The Contract Administration Plan, which provides the framework for effective contract administration.

The Contract Administration Plan (CAP) will vary in scope, complexity, and risk associated with the contract. Non-complex, routine contracts may simply merit a two- or three-page document that discusses specific issues that are worthy of special attention during contract administration.

The frame of the plan should focus on who, what, when, where, and how to administer the contract. Ideally, the plan should be a product of an integrated product team responsible for the monitoring and surveillance of contract performance. To maximize effectiveness, this team must include the contracting representatives and any representatives of technical and other functional areas that have a key stake in the outcome of contract performance. Typical team functions represented may include financial, logistical, and engineering disciplines.

The CAP is the baseline document that governs the contract administration phase, and it should be reviewed and approved by the members of the team. Additionally, a copy of the signed plan should be provided to the contractor. The decision to do so will be an organizational decision. Some public agencies provide the contractor a copy of the plan, while others consider the plan an internal working document. However, a distinct benefit of an open approach to the distribution of the CAP is the clear communication of targeted goals and objectives.

CAPs generally address many or all of the same subjects. The emphasis should be on process, output and outcome, with a particular emphasis on the latter two. Questions such as what, when, who, and how are useful for framing and critically examining the types of information that should be included in the plan. While process may be the primary responsibility of the supplier, an awareness of process by government personnel is valuable, as it can provide important information regarding quality, scheduling, and costs of performance. In other words, public agencies may not be particularly concerned with the "process" a supplier uses to achieve contract goals; rather, emphasis is on achievement of stated outputs and outcomes. Emphasis on process may disengage the Contract Administration Team from the primary goal.

CAPs share a common framework; however, inclusion of each topical area within the CAP should be a matter of need rather than one of formality. Typical components of CAPs will be discussed briefly. Note that it may be beneficial to include each topical area and, where appropriate, state the inapplicability of an area. Doing so will help to avoid an inadvertent omission.

Description. All plans should include an introductory statement that briefly describes the scope of the requirement. This statement often refers the reader to another document or attachment that provides a more in-depth description of the requirement.

Roles and Responsibilities. A critical component of the plan is a list of personnel responsible for specific aspects of contract performance and administration. The roles can include specifically named personnel; or, in some organizations, a designator (e.g., numeric code) may identify the functional title or position within the organization. To ensure that no overlapping responsibilities are delegated, a brief description of each responsibility and what portion of the Statement of Work (SOW) is relevant to the responsibility are necessary. For example, Elaine Carlson may be the quality assurance representative responsible for ensuring the quality of the software program being developed, tested, and installed on the computers within the government office. The relevant portion of the work statement (including reference to the quality standards established in the contract) should be identified.

Period of Performance/Delivery Dates. The plan should include the period of performance of the contract. Options should be clearly identified as well as the conditions and time lines associated with option ordering. Specific dates for the receipt of supplies should also be included.

Data and Deliverables. Specific data requirements and other deliverables should be identified in the CAP. This can be easily accomplished by including the contract data and deliverables information as an attachment to the plan. Frequency of data reporting and deliverables and any contractually mandated quality levels for the data and deliverables should also be included in the plan. Also note the number of copies, format requirements, and the name of the public agency representative responsible for data/deliverable inspection and acceptance.

Specific data requirements and other deliverables should be identified in the CAP.

Testing. Contracts may include testing requirements. These can consist of many scenarios from the complex initial and operational process or performance requirements to beta testing of commercially developed software. Compliance with the established specifications is of particular importance when supplies must operate in an integrated manner. Thus, testing in the operational environment, whether the item is commercial, non-developmental, or full-scale developmental, is an important consideration. Any validation requirements that are stated in the contract should be included or referenced in the CAP. Relevant details about testing should be addressed (e.g., type, evaluation criteria, place, and testing responsibilities).

Inspection and Acceptance. Generally, inspection and acceptance criteria addressed in the contract should be briefly included in the CAP. As stated above, the need to address inspection and acceptance requirements can be included as attachments to the plan. Recognize, however, that if the contract is consistently used as a point of reference throughout the plan, the plan itself serves little purpose because one can simply read the contract. The plan provides a summary of the contract by "highlighting" unusual or critical points that require special attention during contract administration.

Warranty Provisions. A brief statement regarding the type and length of warranty provisions should be included in the plan. If the warranty is other than a standard commercial warranty, specific information regarding the nature of the warranty should be addressed.

Personnel Requirements. Oftentimes, contracts include specific personnel requirements regarding level of education, expertise, and other demonstrations of qualifications. While there is a movement away from providing personnel requirements in contracts, the inclusion of personnel requirements should be stated in the CAP. If the successful proposal includes personnel "promises" in excess of the minimum public agency requirements, the plan should identify such promises. For example, a minimum requirement for a software engineer with a B.S. degree in computer science may be exceeded by the evaluated and selected promise to provide a software engineer with an M.S. in computer science. This is of particular importance when the winning proposal offers a higher price.

Special Terms and Conditions. The plan should mention any special terms and conditions that relate to performance, schedule, and/or cost. For example, a cost type contract may cap overhead rates at a certain level. This is important information for reviewers responsible for the approval of invoices for payment. This section of the plan should be included by title and state "none" if, in fact, no special terms and conditions apply. Doing so will help to avoid the unintended absence of such information.

Watch List Items. Watch lists are contractual-process and outcome-focused initiatives that are on the critical path or have a level of risk or consequence that is unacceptable. Watch list items should be constantly reviewed and updated to ensure that changes to the environmental dynamics have not altered the watch list items or their importance. For example, an interim milestone for successful testing in a simulated environment could be a candidate for the watch list. Once the testing has been successfully completed, the plan would be adjusted to indicate completion of the milestone.

Critical Milestones. Items that are on the critical path are candidates for critical milestone identification. Critical milestones are those interim events that have a direct or indirect impact on the successful completion of the contractual requirements. Remember, contract success can be characterized in broad terms as obtaining a quality product (or service) on time and within budget. As critical milestones are successfully met, the plan is updated to include relevant information.

Schedules and Meetings. Each CAP should contain a schedule of meetings that are to be held throughout the contract. Some meetings can be reasonably predicted and scheduled as a matter of routine. The plan should strive to identify a standard schedule of meetings (e.g., first Tuesday of each month) upon which the stakeholders can rely.

Performance Assessment Plan (PAP)

The Performance Assessment Plan (PAP) is key to successful contract administration. The PAP can be contained within the Contract Administration Plan, or it can be a stand-alone document. The PAP is particularly useful, given the trend toward performance-based contracts. Performance-based contracts focus on output and outcome and leave process to the contractor. The PAP ensures that the public agency is receiving the supplies or services to which it is entitled under the contract.

is based upon the work to be performed by the contractor, as delineated in the of Work, any attachments or exhibits to the Statement of Work, the specifications, 'or's proposal, and any other documents that are contractually binding.

The PAP provides specific information on how the Contract Administration Team will observe and evaluate performance according to the standard required by the contract. Specifically, the PAP includes information on how the "evaluators" will observe, survey, sample, test, evaluate, and document supplier performance.

The PAP is based upon the technical requirements and other relevant terms and conditions to the contract. It is not a contractually binding document, nor is the Contract Administration Plan. The PAP delineates the proposed actions that will be used to evaluate contractor performance. As with any other plan, the PAP is only valuable if it is adopted and implemented. The PAP should be included within the solicitation so that suppliers understand the standard against which they will be evaluated. This is important so that risk and pricing can adequately reflect the standard of performance to be accomplished. A PAP may, in fact, cause a potential supplier to "no bid" work, if the plan is too stringent. Thus, industry standards that have been examined as part of market research often form the foundation of the PAP. The PAP provides potential suppliers with the following information:

- What tasks will be inspected
- When the tasks will be inspected
- What standards will be utilized
- How the evaluation and assessment of performance will be made.

It is important to remember that PAPs are not "one size fits all" documents. The plan must be developed for each procurement. While some components of the plan may transcend specific contracts due to the need for same or similar supplies or services, the dynamics of the operating environment will often cause the details of the plan to change.

Risk is also an important consideration in developing the PAP. The level of performance assessment and the standard to which the contractor will be held affects the degree of risk shared by the contracting parties. The plan should be clear on the metrics to be used, because the plan will often include negative and positive incentives for failure to meet, achieve, and/or exceed performance standards.

The PAP is a dynamic document that should be revised, as necessary, during contract performance. For example, the task and type of performance assessment to be used may prove effective in the first quarter of the contract but may have no relevance to performance requirements in future periods. Accordingly, the plan should clearly state the conditions for revision and enforcement of revised terms.

Effective contract management and surveillance techniques, coupled with the contractor's own quality assurance program, will help to ensure that standards for acceptable or better-than-acceptable performance (as appropriate) are met. A recent trend provides for contractors to submit a proposed PAP with their proposal submission. It is then evaluated as part of the proposal submission, negotiated as appropriate, and used during contract performance by the government performance monitors.

In summary, the PAP provides the who, what, where, when, and how for evaluating performance. Contract managers are cautioned that the best of intentions result in a plan that is impossible to implement due to resource constraints. The key is to determine what is important to the success of the contract so that resources can be focused on those tasks.

Surveillance Techniques

An important component of the PAP is the method and level of surveillance that will be utilized during contract performance to ensure compliance with the standards. If the CAP and the PAP are contained in a single document, the surveillance techniques are a component of the PAP.

A public agency has broad-reaching rights with respect to inspection of services and supplies. These rights are bound by the obligation not to delay or disrupt work while inspection takes place. The agency's inspection rights typically include the right to "inspect any time and any place in a manner that does not delay or disrupt work of the supplier." As a practical matter, the public agency reserves such rights but conducts surveillance in a manner consistent with the level it determines necessary to ensure compliance with contract performance standards.

The purpose of the Surveillance Plan is to develop and adopt a framework for effectively and efficiently conducting systematic surveillance of services. The Surveillance Plan provides for the monitoring and evaluating of all contract requirements. Monitoring is accomplished through a combination of methods:

Sampling. Written procedures should detail what will be checked, the acceptable quality level, lot size, level of surveillance, sample sizes, sampling selection procedures (random, etc.), performance criteria, the evaluation procedure, and the analysis of the results.

The purpose of the Surveillance Plan is to develop and adopt a framework for effectively and efficiently conducting systematic surveillance of services.

Checklists. Checklists are useful methods of ensuring that those responsible for occasional surveillance do not lose sight of specific responsibilities.

Performance Requirement Summary Lists. Such lists identify all contractual activity that is to be monitored and recorded. The lists include the tasks, method of surveillance, standards, acceptable quality levels, and opportunities for relevant remarks of the cognizant inspectors.

Other Information. Contracts may contain unique terms and conditions, which warrant mention as part of surveillance activity. Such terms and conditions may relate to quality assurance clauses, inspection and acceptance clauses, or payment provisions tied to performance standards.

At this point, it is worth examining the terms "insight" and "oversight," because one or both may be a useful means of surveillance. Insight is experiential but relies on intervention by exception rather than as a constraint on the process. Insight is a process-driven approach, which focuses on prevention and improvement—fixing the cause rather than the defect. Oversight is commonly defined as a traditional managerial approach, which involves control, constraints, knowledge, detection, and correction.

Today, insight is viewed as the means to achieve continuous improvement with the end goal of obtaining better suppliers and services at a lower contract price. Insight places responsibility for performance squarely on the contractor rather than on the public agency's surveillance team.

It is important to remember that while process may be important, the primary concern of the surveillance team is to ensure that quality supplies or services are obtained, on time, and at the agreed upon price. The first line of surveillance rests with the contractors who should be required to have in place a quality assurance and Surveillance Plan that ensures that contract performance is in accordance with the standards set forth in the contract.

Surveillance techniques and the surveillance methods delineated in the PAP (or CAP) should focus on those task areas that are critical to the success of contract performance, recognizing any resource constraints that may prevent successful surveillance. A good surveillance methodology will not benefit the agency if it cannot be implemented effectively.

An example of the importance of monitoring and surveillance activities during contract performance can be found in software development efforts. The contractor is often rewarded for software stability improvements, when the software is initially integrated into the operating system. Because software matures over time, it is not possible to identify and remove every possible software "bug" when the software is initially integrated. Therefore, the key performance parameters, which have been established under the contract, must be monitored throughout the integration and testing phases to ensure that the quality and stability goals are met.

Chapter 5

Contract Administration Team:
Roles and Ethical Responsibilities

Introduction

Until now, the procurement professional has been working as the lead person on the contract formation team. After contract award, depending on the size of the agency, the procurement professional may be the only member of the Contract Administration Team or may be a member of a cross-functional Contract Administration Team. The extent of administrative activity required can vary considerably from one contract to another, depending on the complexity of the purchase, the contract type, and the quality of the relationship between the public agency and the contractor and within the Contract Administration Team. One constant requirement for all contracts is the need for effective cooperation and coordination among all personnel in the organization who are involved in the contract administration function. For contract administration to function effectively, it is critical to have a partnership and open communication among the department(s) using the contract and the procurement departments. Within the context of the Contract Administration Team, the purpose of this chapter is to:

- identify the composition of the team
- clarify roles and authority levels/limits of its members
- identify the separation of duties
- review the importance of ethics in contract administration through general guidelines.

Contract Administration Team

Composition of the Team

Depending upon the complexity of the contract, some or all of the following personnel may become involved in contract administration activities.

Contracting Officer (Agent, Buyer, Manager / Supervisor of Procurement). As the Contracting Officer, the role of the procurement agent transitions from being an advisor during the foundation stage of the Statement of Work (SOW) to a decision maker during the bid process and, finally, to coordinator and team member within the Contract Administration Team. Specifically, the Contracting Officer should be responsible for *handling the contractual business relationship with a contractor.*

This means having the responsibility for negotiations, authorizing changes or amendments in the contracting obligations of both parties, entering into any new agreements during the performance of the contract, and settling disputes that arise during contract performance. In representing the business concern of the public agency, the Contracting Officer is also responsible for making sure that both parties meet the terms of the contract. The fundamental role of the Contracting Officer is to protect the interests of the agency. This demands that the Contracting Officer be granted wide latitude to exercise sound business judgment regarding the administration of a contract and must have the authority to coordinate all activities of the team—*coordinating the activities of the different staff members involved in administering a contract.*

Contracting Officer's Representative (COR). This person is typically a representative of the initiating department (an end-user of the product or service) and provides technical guidance to the contractor. (The terms "COR" or "Representative" will be used interchangeably in this text to refer to the Contracting Officer's Representative). The Representative is responsible for providing daily technical oversight of the contract effort when the contract is for one specific department or a specific project. The Representative also has the responsibility for making sure the contractor performs according to the technical requirements of the contract. To accomplish this, the Representative is responsible for the following aspects of contract administration:

- Understanding the requirements of work statements and specifications.
- Converting requirements into specifications and drawings.
- Assisting in the preparation and maintenance of all the statements of work.
- Chairing design reviews.
- Providing technical guidance to the contractor and monitoring all day-to-day and technical interfaces with the contractor.

- Serving as the focal point for all correspondence and directions concerning technical direction.
- Ensuring that all technical direction is recorded in writing.
- Maintaining a file of all technical instructions that are issued as well as all deliverables received.
- Bringing to the attention of the contractor any inefficient or wasteful methods being used on contracts that are not fixed price.
- Ensuring that the goods or services received are in accordance with the contract.
- Keeping the Contracting Officer informed of significant events involving the contract.

Subject Matter Expert. This person provides expertise on technical aspects of a highly complex project and may or may not be a member of the end-user department. For example, if the focus of the contract is to implement a comprehensive data management system for the agency, it may be helpful to have an objective expert in computer technology join the team with no formal ties to either the agency or the contractor.

Quality Assurance Specialist. This person ensures that the contractor has an acceptable quality plan, provides on-site inspection and acceptance of goods and/or services, and coordinates quality problems and waivers with the designer or design engineer.

Reliability Engineer. This person ensures that reliability requirements are suitable for the procurement at hand and that the contractor complies with the established requirements. The Reliability Engineer establishes the level of reliability for the hardware being purchased, generates reliable documents, and approves contractor-generated documents.

Material and Services Price and Cost Analyst. This person assists the Contract Administrator in preparing the analyses and evaluations of contractor submittals and assists the Contract Administrator if change orders require cost analysis.

Legal Counsel. This person advises anyone who provides status, rules, statistics, or other related issues.

In the case of extremely large procurement projects, the following representatives may also be included on the public agency's team.

Program Office Representative. This person provides direction and assistance to the contractor through the following possible responsibilities: preparing schedules, reporting, controlling activities through the contract administrator, maintaining the internal schedule and cost control for the program in coordination with appropriate sales personnel. The Program Office Representative may be the interface between the procurement organization and the ultimate customer.

On-site Representative. This person attends contractor status meetings and provides or assistance for quality, engineering, shortage, and cost problems.

Clarifying Roles and Establishing Authority Levels and Limits

The respective roles and responsibilities of the Contract Administration Team should be established early so each member of the team understands their authority, the limits to such authority, and the importance of communication and coordination of activities within the team. The two primary authority levels are (1) determining who is leading the daily management of the contract and (2) who makes the final decisions.

A key element of effective contract administration is making certain that each member of the Contract Administration Team knows the other members' roles and clearly understands who has been given authority to act on behalf of the public agency within these two primary authority levels. While these professionals work together as a team, and complement and support each other's efforts, it is important that there be no confusion regarding who is responsible for which activities and who has the authority to take certain actions.

Frequently, problems arise when personnel unilaterally exceed their authority in offering decisions, guidance, or instructions to a contractor, further keeping this information from the team. For effective contract management, there can be no room for such "surprises." It is tough enough to manage the relationship with a contractor without having to contend with an undisciplined and uncoordinated team.

Accordingly, effective contract management requires a cross-functional, team-based approach to contract administration. Clear communication of all operating activities by means of reports, charts, and status meetings are key characteristics of a successful cross-functional team. Problem areas must be brought to the Contract Administration Team's attention in a timely manner, and solutions or "work-arounds" should be activated, i.e., plans to complete other tasks until the required material arrives or activities are complete. The Contracting Officer's Representative must be willing to offer help and suggestions and share the consequences, if necessary. The contractor must also have some freedom to manage its position without undue interference.

Separation of Duties

The role of Contracting Officials in contract administration, when performed properly, represents a critically important management function. Contract Administration Teams experience problems when individual members circumvent the responsibilities of the Contracting Officers. For example, valuable resources are lost when the Contracting Officer's Representative inappropriately, though perhaps unknowingly, asks a contractor to perform outside of the scope of work specified in a contract.

For this reason, there is a need to establish and maintain a clear separation of duties between contracting personnel and the project staff. This is often difficult to accomplish. The

Contracting Officer should be the only official who can authorize the public agency to take any action that affects the contractual business relationship with the contractor.

Many actions will be based on the recommendations of the Contracting Officer's Representative, and there should be strong discipline over the contract administration process. The Contracting Officer should formally ratify suggestions of the Contracting Officer's Representative, who is working most closely with the contractor. This system of "checks and balances" is an important element in protecting the public agency's fundamental business interests and should not be minimized.

To avoid confusion as to the respective authority or personnel, there should be written documentation or policies establishing the roles, responsibilities, and authority of those involved in dealing with the contractor. The written notices should be signed by appropriate senior officials and maintained in the official contract files.

If there is an opportunity for confusion among team player authority and responsibility, chances are it will occur between the Contracting Officer and the Contracting Officer's Representative. The text describes the perfect world for both positions. In actuality the Contracting Officer will need to be sensitive to internal politics, the complexity of the project, and how comfortable the Contracting Officer is with the expertise of the Representative.

In turn, successful contract administration will also depend on the cooperation and contributions of the other professionals mentioned above, particularly the Representative. As stated previously, there needs to be a single source of authority for authorizing actions that reflect the formal business relationship between the organization and a contractor. This authority should rest with the Contracting Officer, which may cause conflict between the Contracting Officer and the Representative, because the COR works closely with the vendor after the contract award and may view the Contracting Officer's actions as interference. Nevertheless, it is important for the Representative to recognize the limits of their authority.

- The COR cannot modify the stated terms of the contract unilaterally via a change order or amendment. Only the Contracting Officer has this authority. Change authority levels may be clearly stated in the RFQ or RFP document, which, in turn, will become a part of the final contract.

- The COR cannot direct the contractor to start or stop work unless authorized in writing by the Contracting Officer to do so.

- The COR cannot direct the contractor to perform work not specified in the contract without adequate documents agreed to by both parties.

- The COR cannot approve items of cost not authorized by the contract.

- The COR cannot execute any supplemental agreement amendments.

- The COR cannot render any decisions on contractual disputes or questions of fact.

Ethics in Contract Administration

As civil servants and stewards of public dollars, it is critical that public agency employees who are engaged in any aspect of the acquisition and contracting function subscribe to the highest standards of ethical behavior. This section will discuss the general attributes of effective ethical standards and will then apply these standards to the Contract Administration Team.

General Guidelines

The ABA's (2001) *2000 Model Procurement Code for State and Local Governments Regulation* 12-204 (1) defines public employee conflict of interest as:

> (1) Conflict of Interest. It shall be a breach of ethical standards for any employee to participate directly or indirectly in a procurement when the employee knows that:
> (a) the employee or any member of the employee's immediate family has a financial interest pertaining to the procurement;
> (b) a business or organization in which the employee, or any member of the employee's immediate family, has a financial interest pertaining to the procurement; or
> (c) any other person, business, or organization that has an arrangement concerning prospective employment is involved in the procurement.

A conflict of interest occurs when judgment, action, or non-action taken by a team member benefits the same member. Within the context of this issue, there are three types of conflict of interest generally recognized by the public procurement profession.

Actual Conflict of Interest. This occurs when a decision or action would be compromised without taking appropriate action to eliminate the conflict. If the employee has an outside interest that conflicts with their public responsibilities to the extent that their public responsibilities or decisions are influenced to the detriment of the public or the benefit of the employee or their personal interest, a conflict of interest is created. Such action may include the employee receiving a direct or indirect financial benefit as a result of using their public position and/or influence; or the outside influence could be so prevalent that the public decision is influenced or dictated by the employee's outside interest.

Potential Conflict of Interest. This is a situation where the employee has outside, private influ-   nd/or interests that could influence public decisions, actions, or responsibilities.
         from an actual conflict of interest in that actions have yet to occur where the
         ence and/or interests of the employee affect or dictate public decisions, actions,
         lities.

Appearance of a Conflict of Interest. This is any situation in which a reasonable person would conclude that the employee has an outside influence and/or interest, which conflicts with their public duties or responsibilities.

Public Employee Conflict of Interest

The following actions by any public employee are generally deemed to be a conflict of interest.

- Use or attempted use of the public employee's official position to secure benefits, privileges, exemptions, or advantages to the employee, the employee's immediate family, or an organization with which the employee is associated that are different from those available to the general public.

- Acceptance of other employment or contractual relationship that will affect the public employee's independence of judgment in the exercise of official duties.

- Action as an agent or attorney in any action or matter pending before the employing agency except in the proper discharge of official duties or on the employee's behalf.

A conflict of interest occurs when judgment, action, or non-action taken by a team member benefits the same member.

Resolving Conflict of Interest Issues

Each public agency should establish a policy creating an internal mechanism for employees' use in identifying an actual conflict of interest or a potential conflict of interest. Notice of this policy should be disseminated throughout the public agency and should minimally include the following two provisions:

Immediate Action. A public agency or employee must immediately act upon any suggestion, inquiry, or intimation that an actual conflict of interest exists. Upon identification, such matters should be referred to the agency ethics officer and to a supervisor, manager, director, assistant commissioner, or agency head. It is appropriate for small agencies having no internal auditors or human resources staff to refer suspected conflicts to the Department of Procurement.

Transfer Responsibility, if Conflict Exists. If a public agency employee, s¹ manager, appointing authority, or agency head determines that a potential conflict exists, as defined by policy or relevant law, responsibilities for the contract administration function must be assigned to an employee having no conflict of interest. If the agency head determines that assigning those duties to another employee within the agency is not possible, they must contact top management who will assist in finding personnel to perform the contract administration function.

Each public employee (*or any individual involved in the contract administration function*), as an individual, is responsible for NOT putting himself or herself and his or her public agency in a position where a conflict of interest may, might, or could give the appearance of conflict. When an employee believes the potential for a conflict of interest exists, it is the employee's duty to avoid the situation.

Applying Ethical Standards to Non-Public Agency Personnel

Public agencies should consider establishing a policy for non-public agency personnel who participate in the contract administration process, as many agencies routinely use non-public agency personnel, such as expert consultants, to assist in creating and evaluating bids and proposals and in making contract award recommendations. (In some cases, legislation may dictate the participation of representatives from certain groups.)

Ideally, a policy should be implemented that requires non-public agency personnel to read, understand, and agree to be bound by the mandates of the statutes and policies relevant to their participation in the contract administration process. A record of this agreement should be kept with the official agency copy of activity related to the resulting contract. To protect the public agency, its agencies and employees, everyone involved in the acquisition and contract administration process must be held to the same standards.

Specific Guidelines for the Contract Administration Team

The Contracting Officer needs to set an example for ethical performance and recognize what constitutes a conflict of interest. Opportunities for conflict of interest will present themselves. How to deal with conflict of interest is the focus of this section.

The appearance or perception of a conflict of interest between the contractor and any of the Contract Administration Team members continually plagues the perception of the public agency by the general public. For this reason, team personnel must be alert to situations that may create a real or perceived conflict of interest. Ethics and integrity cannot be understated to protect the trust between members of the Contract Administration Team and the general public.

The Contracting Officer should determine the best time and place to review the issue of ethics. Consider reviewing ethical issues at the start of team development as part of the first meeting when discussing the SOW. An alternate time may be the first Contract Administration Team meeting subsequent to the execution of the contract, at a time when all the parties are together to discuss the daily responsibilities of each. Team members in daily contact with the contractor and the contractor's representatives will be made aware of the ethics-based parameters that they must follow during the several months or years of working together. Members of the Contract Administration Team must:

- be familiar with any code of ethics published by the public agency
- refuse gifts and gratuities from the contractor
- avoid any appearance of a conflict of interest with the contractor, such as accepting any activity that is paid for by the contractor (e.g., lunches, golf outings, sports events)
- be aware that having financial ties to the contractor's business (stocks) is not acceptable, unless it is part of a deferred compensation mutual fund.

Each member of the Contract Administration Team should complete a Conflict of Interest form (Appendix A), which should be retained in the contract file.

References

American Bar Association (2001). *2000 model procurement code for state and local governments.* Regulation 12-204 (pp. 91-92). Washington, DC: American Bar Association.

State of Minnesota (1998). *Contract decision guidelines, ethics and conflict of interest.* Saint Paul: State of Minnesota, Department of Administration, Materials Management Division.

Chapter 6

Initial Contract Administration Activities

With the Contract Administration Team in place, the public agency should now focus on those post-award activities that should be conducted shortly after the contract is executed between the public agency and the contractor. This chapter will discuss how the following activities affect contract administration:

- post award activities to include debriefings and start-up conferences
- critical areas for contract monitoring
- effective contract control
- contract files.

Post-Award Activities

Debriefing of all Bidders responding to the Bid or Proposal

Depending on the dollar amount of the contract and its complexity, debriefing of all bidders who responded to the solicitation may save time and dollars associated with contract award protests. The adage "one ounce of prevention is worth a pound of cure" applies. Whether the meeting(s) should be held prior to or subsequent to contract execution is debatable. Based on prior experience, the Contract Officer has the final decision as to when to conduct the debriefings. The Contract Officer will establish the time and place of the meeting, coordinating with all of the interested parties and the agency's personnel who are expected to attend.

Often, the debriefing occurs before or during the time a contract is being assembled for signature. For competitive sealed bids, a summary of bid prices is assembled and distributed just prior to meeting with a responding bidder. During the meeting, the Contracting Officer responds to vendor questions about the bid process. For competitive sealed proposals, separate discussions are held with each bidder. The Contracting Officer discusses how the proposal was scored and answers any questions specific only to the bidder's proposal. Should debriefings occur prior to award, the other proposals and pricing are discussed only after the award has been made.

The bidder's participation in the debriefing at the minimum might include the person(s) signing the bid and the bidder's proposed project lead. Persons representing the public agency should minimally include the Contract Officer, and the Technical Project Officer. The bidders usually welcome debriefings conducted in open, honest communications.

Post-Award Start-Up Conferences with the Awarded Contractor

The decision to conduct a post-award conference depends on the following variables:

- size and complexity of the project
- contract type
- urgency of the project
- contractor's performance history.

In most situations, it is very beneficial to hold a post-award conference attended by personnel from both parties to the contract. After the contract has been executed, it is time to discuss contract performance expectations with the Contract Administration Team. Attendees should include all members of the public agency's Contract Administration Team and their corresponding contractor counterparts. A post-award conference ensures that the contractor understands the expectations, performs accordingly, and can provide the foundation for an effective contract effort. If it is determined after a contract award that the contractor does not or may not have a clear understanding of the scope of the contract, the technical requirements, or the rights and obligations of each party, it is essential that the public agency initiate appropriate actions to clarify any ambiguities and resolve any misunderstandings.

The basic objectives of a post-award conference are to:

- make sure the contractor understands the technical requirements of the contract
- clarify the rights and responsibilities of both parties
- determine the need for a follow-up meeting.

During the post-award conference, the Contracting Officer should provide leadership in reviewing the following issues:

- the public agency's mission and objective and how they relate to the contract
- restating the promises made by both parties in the contract language
- any special contract provisions
- identification of all individuals authorized to make decisions or modifications regarding the contract
- the procedures that will be followed in monitoring the contractor's effort (inducing any quality control and testing requirements, time sheets, reports required and when, etc.)
- any approach to quality control that the contractor plans to use
- any incentive features included in the contract
- the reporting requirements the contractor is expected to meet
- payment procedures
- any subcontracting issues
- delivery
- hazardous material or operations and safety precautions required.

...it is very beneficial to hold a post-award conference attended by personnel from both parties to the contract.

Following the post-award conference, the Contracting Officer should produce a formal report summarizing the major issues and should identify any issues not resolved or requiring additional action. The report should be distributed to everyone who attended the meeting and to any other appropriate personnel.

Critical Areas for Monitoring by the Contract Administration Team

Chapter 3 mentioned that anticipating the typical contract administration problems that can occur and developing contract goals could manage risk. Each type of purchase has typical contract administration problems associated with it. A graph included in Chapter 3 has been repeated as Figure 7 due to the critical nature of monitoring for these types of problems.

General Contract Type	Wrong Product	Delays	Definition of Acceptance	Change Order	Conflict	Other Sources	Poor Performance	Risk of Failure/ Terminate	Sub Contractors	Cost
Supplies and Small Purchases	X	X								
Capital Outlay	X	X						X		X
Professional Services (e.g. Architects)		X	X	X	X	X				
Contracted Services (e.g. Custodial)			X	X	X		X	X	X	
Software		X	X	X		X	X	X	X	
Leases				X	X	X	X			
Construction		X		X	X	X		X	X	X

Figure 7. Contract Administration Problems Related to Specific Types of Contracts

The following areas should be specifically addressed in the contract document and then monitored and managed by the team, as appropriate, based on the risk to the agency.

- quality or incorrect item received
- schedules: dates when certain activities will be completed (delays)
- acceptance
- contract changes and need for contract amendments
- conflict between vendor and agency
- data management (if applicable)
- contractor performance
- budget allocation and payment
- risk of failure
- subcontractors.

Monitoring Quality

Quality assurance is an important aspect of contract management. Appropriate reporting from the quality assurance department and representation by its personnel at status meetings are mandatory. An undue number of problems in the area of quality tend to cause both schedule slippage and cost deterioration. Quality must be managed carefully to prevent an adverse impact on the other operating areas. Different contract types will require different emphasis and skill sets to determine adequate quality. For example, a single individual may be able to determine if adequate quality has been achieved in small purchases and capital outlay purchases, but a team may be needed to determine if a professional service, contracted service, software acquisition, or construction project has achieved the desired quality level.

Monitoring Schedules

After the post-award conference, *all schedules of deliverables* must be detailed and finalized, including important milestones that are critical for the successful completion of the project. For instance, a buyer who contracts for the construction of a building must establish dates by which all activities must be completed. Walls cannot be constructed until the foundation is poured, and the framing must be completed before the electrical work can be started. The same is true for any large project. Planning and control charts should be created and completion dates established.

Monitoring Acceptance

Often, agencies will drag their feet on final acceptance because the specifications are not complete and additional work is required to complete the contract. This type of delay can be a key source of conflict between the contractor and the Contracting Officer's Representative. If the contractor has completed the work identified in the specifications, the public agency should accept the work. If it has been determined that the agency will require additional work to complete the project, the agency should either issue a change order under the existing contract or begin work on developing specifications and contractual terms under a new solicitation for Phase II.

Monitoring Changes

It is essential for the Contracting Officer to develop a comprehensive system to control contract changes. A contract control system should require appropriate justification and allow appropriate timing to process each requested change. The ability to issue a unilateral change must be specified in the contract. Specific instructions should be in place that control the level of the change, who can approve it, the costs involved, and appropriate feedback to all team members who need it. Examples of contracts requiring constant monitoring are construction and software contracts.

Monitoring Conflicts

Poorly written specifications are the most common cause of conflicts within the Contract Administration Team and between the team and the contractor. The Contracting Officer must be proactive in anticipating the potential for conflicts and should intervene and render decisions, when appropriate. Any contract with a significant *human* component has the potential for conflicts, such as professional and contracted services agreements.

Managing contractor performance is one of the basic responsibilities for the Contract Administration Team.

Monitoring Data

Contracts containing large amounts of report data should be tracked closely by using a detailed schedule of deliverables, delivery milestones, and a good reporting system.

Monitoring Contractor Performance

Managing contractor performance is one of the basic responsibilities for the Contract Administration Team. The contractor and the public agency have made specific contractual promises in writing. The contractor must be held accountable to perform at acceptable levels. The team will determine if performance has deteriorated to the point of invoking a time period for cure or invoking remedies. The contractor should hold the public agency responsible for contractual promises as well.

A word about contractor performance reviews is appropriate. Most programs of any size require that both formal and informal reviews be done at both the contractor and agency's facilities. At a minimum, the following basic guidelines are important when conducting performance reviews. Performance reviews should be conducted at least quarterly during the contract period.

- The review should provide a status report of the contractor's performance in the areas of costs, schedules, and technical activities.

- Normally, the Contract Officer conducts reviews with support from the contract team, as necessary.

- All reviews should be scheduled in advance, and all participants should be provided with an agenda.

- Action items should be gathered and assigned with required completion dates. Follow-up for closure should not wait until the next review but should be assigned to a member of the team for regular status reports. The updated status of each action item should be reviewed by the Contract Officer at the next meeting.

If an item falls behind between meetings, the Contract Officer must work with the appropriate personnel to obtain closure.

- Material hazards should be addressed during the review. The Contract Officer should attempt to alert all affected personnel of new hazards before the review so that they can provide an appropriate recovery plan at the meeting.

Details discussed at these meetings should never be left to memory, because each participant may remember them somewhat differently. Minutes should be distributed to all attendees as well as other interested individuals. In addition to an "action items" listing, minutes should be recorded and published for all meetings.

The specific method chosen to manage a contract is not as important as the implementation of sufficient controls to achieve the desired results. Trained and competent personnel are the most important ingredients in successful contract monitoring.

Monitoring the Budget and Payment

The next task is to monitor payments within the established *budgets* for each activity. Consideration should be given to allocating additional funds in reserve for contract changes that are necessary due to unanticipated development problems or unforeseen environmental conditions. These situations can frequently occur in construction, professional services, or software contracts. Budgets and payments should be established and reviewed periodically for any necessary adjustments. In addition, budgets must be reallocated if work is modified or changed from one area or department to another. Budgets should be closely tracked using written reports to ensure that problem areas are given timely attention. If problems are neglected, overruns may be noticed much too late for effective corrective action to be taken. This is particularly critical in contracts having several implementation phases.

Monitoring Risk of Failure

Certain contracts will have a higher risk of failure due to any of the following factors; new technology, sole source, tight delivery schedules, high cost. The team will have to develop a monitoring plan that anticipates any potential problems and have a plan in place to deal with delays.

Monitoring Subcontractors

If subcontractors are used, the team will have to develop a monitoring plan that addresses any potential problems in communication.

Effective Contract Control

The Contracting Officer is responsible for providing leadership and expertise in the contract administration process. The Contracting Officer should provide expertise in contract control. Contract control is the process of "making it happen." The contract control process involves three key ingredients: (1) developing a performance plan; (2) monitoring the performance to date; and (3) anticipating the actions required to make things happen.

Developing a Performance Plan

The Contract Administration Team should develop a performance plan before the contractor begins the project. The team should determine what specific critical components within the contract should be monitored, how monitoring is going to occur, who is going to perform the monitoring functions, and when the monitoring will begin. Many of these activities can be determined through previous contract administration experiences.

How the public agency makes decisions regarding any aspect of contract administration is critical. Time constraints are not a reason for overlooking poor vendor contract performance. The following are some additional issues to consider in an effort to proactively avoid a more serious situation:

- The public agency, not the contractor, must retain control over the contract. It is important to monitor the contractor's performance and compliance to the contractual promises.

- Watch the time limits. Is the contractor in compliance with the performance milestones? What actions are going to be taken if they are not?

- Do not create an employer-employee relationship. The public agency does not work for the contractor but is in partnership with the contractor to accomplish the tasks.

- The contract may have a recruitment prohibition clause prohibiting each from recruiting employees of the other for a period of time.

- Institutional memory must reside with the public agency and not the contractor. Keep good documentation and minutes of meetings with the contractor.

- Contractors should not represent the public agency before a governing body, such as a commission, legislature, or council, with the exception of some professional services.

Monitoring the Performance to Date

Often, the Contracting Officer waits until it is too late to take effective corrective measures. A seemingly innocent delay can cause a ripple effect, such as an inadequate foundation for a building. This is why milestone monitoring is so important! With this information, a manager can monitor a task or schedule and begin to work on a recovery plan before the entire project is late. Important matters must be specified in writing. Copies of correspondence to the proper individuals prove very helpful in effecting overall contract control.

Anticipating the Actions Required to Make Things Happen

A delay in one area may adversely affect another area. A change order to correct a short-term problem may cause long-term problems later. Once the Contract Officer receives the reports, they must be reviewed for necessary actions. All Contract Administration Team members should receive copies of specific reports that deal with issues in their areas of responsibility so they can be of assistance in controlling and directing necessary "work-arounds" or solutions to problems that have arisen. An item often neglected is the simple matter of correspondence. When contractors send letters to the Contracting Officer's Representative, an appropriate response requires input from other team members. To remain aware of these matters, the Representative should maintain a log of open correspondence and require status reports at weekly or bi-weekly program reviews. A program correspondence log can take many forms.

How public agencies make decisions regarding any aspects of contract administration is critical. Because the public is allowed to review and question the expenditure of public funds, a strict set of standards and guidelines should be followed.

Contract Files

As mentioned throughout this text, the critical function of managing contracts through effective documentation is essential to a successful contract administration program. A checklist of contract documents is provided below as a reference:

- The executed contract, related bid documents, and Notice of Award
- Required bonds and insurance certificates and any correspondence with surety companies
- Conflict of Interest form, completed by each member of the Contract Administration Team
- Post-award documentation from or to the contractor

- Notice to proceed
- Approvals or disapprovals of contract submittals required by the contract and requests for waivers or deviations from contractual requirements
- Documentation of performance monitoring
- Modifications/changes to the contract, including the rationale for the change order and whether the request for change was issued or denied
- Documentation regarding any changes in the delivery date or contract price as a result of the changes
- Documentation regarding the settlement of claims and disputes, including, as appropriate, results of audit, legal reviews of the claims, and approval by the proper authority of the settlement amount
- Documentation regarding "stop work" and "suspension of work" orders and termination actions
- Documentation of inspection and acceptance
- Documentation of contract closeout

References

Cavinato, J. L., Ph.D., C.P.M., & Kauffman, R. G., Ph.D., C.P.M., National Association of Purchasing Management (NAPM) (2000). *The purchasing handbook* (6th ed.). New York: McGraw-Hill Trade.

National Association of State Procurement Officials (NASPO) (1987). *Contract cookbook for purchase of services*. Lexington, KY: NASPO.

State of Minnesota (1997, September 30). *Contract management training.* Saint Paul: State of Minnesota.

Thai, K. V., Ph.D. (2007). *Introduction to public procurement (2nd ed.).* Herndon, VA: NIGP.

Part III: Contract Administration Concepts and Applications

Chapter 7

Inspection and Acceptance

Introduction

As stated earlier, the broad goals of contract administration are to successfully complete the procurement of a particular good or service by assuring that the public agency receives the needed services or goods on time, in the right quantity, of the right quality, and the contractor is properly compensated. Several of the typical contract administration problems involve delays in delivery and compliance with quality specifications.

Acceptance and rejection techniques are used by the public agency to apply the quality specifications of a contract. These techniques are a part of the overall contract monitoring process that was highlighted in chapter 6. The inspection and acceptance clauses are included in contracts to give the public agency the right to monitor specification compliance and take action when necessary. This chapter will discuss:

- The obligations and rights of both parties with regard to inspection
- The types of inspection and testing methods to verify
  compliance with contract specifications
- Quality assurance programs
- Documentation requirements in conjunction with
  the receiving and inspection process
- Methods for proper acceptance
- Remedies for defects
- Rights and limitations of rejection
- Post acceptance rights related to latent defects,
  fraud, gross mistakes, and warranties.

Obligations of both Parties with Regard to Inspection

Inspection ensures that the contract is fully performed by guaranteeing that the product or service is received in the correct quality, correct quantity, and in a timely manner. After satisfactory inspection, the product or service should be granted final acceptance. After a product or service is accepted, the public agency has limited rejection rights. Proper receiving and inspection methods are critical components of contract administration that provide for the early detection of defects and allow for corrective action to be taken. A standard inspection clause should address the following responsibilities for each party:

- public agency's right to inspect
- allowance for testing
- cost of inspection
- place of inspection
- time of inspection

Public Agency's Right to Inspect

The buyer's legal right to inspect goods is stated in the Uniform Commercial Code (U.C.C.), Section 2-513(1):

> (1) Unless otherwise agreed and subject to subsection (3), where goods are tendered or delivered or identified to the contract for sale, the buyer has a right before payment or acceptance to inspect them at any reasonable place and time and in any reasonable manner. When the seller is required or authorized to send the goods to the buyer, the inspection may be after their arrival.

Based on this right of the buyer (in this case, the public agency), all contracts should contain an inspection clause providing the public agency with broad rights to inspect the contractor's work. An example of an inspection clause is paragraph (c) of the U.S. Government's Federal Acquisition Regulations (FAR) 52.246-2 entitled "The Inspection of Supplies, Fixed Price," which states:

> The Government has the right to inspect and test all supplies called for by the contract, to the extent practicable, at all places and times, including the period of manufacture, and in any event before acceptance. The Government shall perform inspections and tests in a manner that will not unduly delay the work. The Government assumes no contractual obligation to perform any inspection and test for the benefit of the Contractor unless specifically set forth elsewhere in this contract.

The right to inspect does not create a duty for the public agency to inspect, and the failure to conduct an inspection does not relieve the contractor of the responsibility to meet the specifications.

Cost of Inspection

Each party is responsible for costs of the inspections and tests it conducts. The contractor is liable for the public agency's re-inspection costs, if the product fails any inspection test due to the fault of the contractor. The standard FAR 52.246-2(d) supply contract inspection clause includes language requiring the contractor to pay the costs that can reasonably be foreseen at the time of entering into the contract that are necessary to facilitate inspection:

> If the Government performs inspection or test on the premises of the Contractor or Sub-Contractor, the Contractor shall furnish, and shall require Sub-Contractors to furnish without additional charge, all reasonable facilities and assistance for the safe and convenient performance of these duties. Except as otherwise provided in the contract, the Government shall bear the expense of Government inspections or tests made at other than the Contractor's premises; provided, that in case of rejection, the Government shall not be liable for any reduction in the value of inspection or test samples.

Allowance for Testing

The contract should allow for testing in order to provide for the acceptance of products and services. There are two general categories of testing.

Contractually-Specified Testing. The contract may contain testing specifications that will be conducted prior to acceptance. If a test is specified, a level of performance has been established and the public agency may not impose a different test that may require the product or service to meet a higher standard of performance. If a particular test is required for one part of the specifications, the public agency is allowed to conduct other tests, either specified or unspecified, to determine compliance with the remaining specifications.

Unspecified Testing. Unspecified testing may be used as a basis for acceptance or rejection if the test is calculated reasonably and accurately to determine specification compliance. The key is to have adequate specifications that describe a standard of performance. Unspecified tests cannot impose a greater standard of performance. Subjective tests influenced by personal beliefs or feelings are allowed if the subjective tests conform to generally accepted industry practices.

Place of Inspection

A standard inspection clause should grant the public agency the ability to inspect the product or service at any place. Inspection may occur at multiple locations. If it does, acceptance at only one location does not translate into final acceptance. Certain contracts, such as contracts for construction or complex equipment fabrication, may require the inspection of components at the point of manufacture for the purpose of determining suitability of the component and final inspection of the finished product. If a place of inspection is specified and then changed, the public agency may be responsible for any increases in the contractor's cost due to the change in location.

Time of Inspection

The inspection clause grants the public agency the ability to inspect the product or service at any time, but it may not unreasonably interfere with the contractor's ability to perform. Acceptance based on inspection must occur within a reasonable time. If a time of inspection is specified and then changed, the public agency may be responsible for any increases in the contractor's cost due to the change in the time of inspection.

Inspection and Testing Methods to Verify Compliance with Contract Specifications

The public agency's receiving and inspection function may be centralized or decentralized. Centralized receiving occurs when all packages are shipped to one location and inspected by one department. Decentralized receiving occurs when packages are shipped to the end-user and the end-user has responsibility for inspection. It is crucial in either environment that all receiving and inspection personnel implement consistent receiving and inspection practices.

The... receiving and inspection function may be centralized or decentralized.

Once the public agency receives delivery, it must ensure that the items conform to the requirements of the contract. The public agency's receiving procedures and the contract documents define the receiving process. Inspection of received items may be limited to receiving personnel looking for shipping damage, counting the quantities, and noting the items received. Conversely, some purchases require additional inspections. A product or service may require technical inspection or sampling inspection based on the criticality of quality characteristics and/or the economics of the situation.

The following inspection techniques can be used by a public agency to verify that the equipment, services, or construction items conform to the specifications and other requirements.

Exception Inspection

Inspection by exception assumes performance is acceptable until a complaint is lodged. The public agency expends few resources when this inspection method is used. This inspection method is cost effective when purchasing standard off-the-shelf items, such as commercially produced products. This method has several potential dangers, however. Non-conforming products may be accepted and services may be completed prior to the discovery of a defect, potentially diminishing the value of the service provided.

After-Delivery Inspection

This method is used for the inspection of maintenance, repair, operating supplies, and commercial goods and products, such as office supplies, lumber, and electrical supplies. These items are low value and high volume, and commercial standards exist for these products. Inspection is conducted at the public agency's site after the contractor delivers the items and prior to use, to ensure compliance with specifications and contractual agreements. Inspection of received items may be limited to receiving personnel looking for shipping damage, counting the quantities, and matching the items received with the packing list.

In-Process Inspection

This inspection method is used to inspect items at the contractor's site while work is in progress to ensure that the current production or "work-to-date" complies with specifications and contractual agreements.

Final Inspection

Final inspection involves the examination of an item to ensure conformity to all applicable specifications and requirements before making final payment. This inspection usually occurs in construction, customized heavy equipment, technology purchases, software, and service contracts.

Sampling Inspection

Inspection by sampling is effective when purchasing large quantities of items that ~an be divided into smaller lots; or when it is necessary to test a sample by destroyir Determining the sample lot size, the number of acceptable defects, and the level of t will have an impact on the sampling method and frequency of testing. There are two basic sampling techniques.

The **Attribute Sampling** technique for inspection is an "either-or" proposition—an item is either acceptable or unacceptable because it has or lacks specified characteristics. Office supplies are typically sampled in this manner.

The **Variable Sampling** technique for inspection provides for acceptance within certain tolerances based on predetermined factors. This technique is suitable for use when testing for compliance with performance specifications.

The choice of either type of inspection should be based on how critical the quality characteristics are and the economics of the inspection. Most purchasers conduct inspections on an attribute basis. These inspections generally are quicker and less expensive than those based on variables.

Entire lots may be rejected if the number of defects in the sample lot is exceeded. On the other hand, the entire lot will be accepted if the predetermined number of defects is not exceeded. The public agency may re-inspect and reject individual items of accepted lots.

Technical Testing through Laboratories

Frequently, technical inspections require complex technical testing. In these cases, the contract should provide specific details of the testing requirements. The public agency may conduct the testing internally or contract with a laboratory. In other circumstances, the supplier may be required to provide certificates from independent laboratories. Some state and large local governments have testing facilities that can be used for checking compliance. Others have cooperative arrangements with other state and local governments, universities, and/or departments of transportation or agriculture that have such facilities.

If a public agency decides to use an independent laboratory, it may develop an initial list of firms having the required capability by reviewing trade indices or journals, discussing options with peers in government or academia, or contacting trade associations such as the American Council of Independent Laboratories, Inc. (Washington, DC) or the Canadian Testing Association (Ottawa). The public agency may also review American Society for Testing and Materials (ASTM) or American National Standards Institute (ANSI) directories and publications for commercial standards. Finally, the public agency may request a list of independent laboratories accredited by the National Institute of Standards and Technology (Gaithersburg, MD) under its National Voluntary Laboratory Accreditation Program. Evaluation and selection of a laboratory is similar to evaluation and selection of any supplier. Because the organization makes critical decisions based on the laboratory test results, the organization must have confidence in a laboratory's ability to provide accurate test results.

First-Article Testing

First-article testing demonstrates the contractor's ability to produce the desired good or service by testing the first item or "article" produced by the contractor for compliance with specifications. The public agency may require this type of testing when the contractor has never produced this item or when the contract contains performance specifications, such as required for military weapons. The first-article test establishes a level of performance for only that stage of production. The contractor is still responsible for complying with the remaining specifications.

Prevention vs. Detection

Defect-prevention strategies typically are more effective and efficient than defect-detection approaches. Prevention methods use statistically analyzed data to predict and control process behavior. The most common of these approaches is referred to as Statistical Process Control (SPC), a technique used to identify the impending production of an unacceptable product before it actually occurs. This prevention method makes it possible to control quality before or during the first stages of production, thereby improving productivity. When the causes for the defect are identified, they can be corrected, and the process can be stabilized or brought "under control."

A statistical process control system is one of the key building blocks used in implementing a strategy of "continuous improvement" and is the focus of quality management in today's public agency environment. Continuous improvement requires the ability to improve the basic capabilities of the production process by eliminating defects before they occur (FAR 46.202-3, GSA Federal Standard 368A).

Contractor Quality Assurance Certification

Another example of a quality assurance program is ISO 9000. ISO 9000 is a series of standards developed and published by the International Organization for Standardization (ISO) that define, establish, and maintain an effective quality system for manufacturing and service industries. It serves many different industries and organizations as a guide to quality products, services, and management. An organization can be ISO-9000-certified if it successfully follows the ISO 9000 standards for its industry. In order to be certified, the organization must submit to an examination by an outside assessor. The assessor interviews staff members to ensure that they understand their responsibilities for complying with the ISO 9000 standard. The assessor also examines the organization's written documentation to ensure ISO 9000 compliance. The assessor then prepares a detailed report that describes the components of the standard that the organization did not meet. The organization then agrees to correct any problems within a specific time frame. When all problems are corrected, the organization can then be certified. Today, there are approximately 350,000 ISO-9000-certified organizations in over 150 countries.

Documentation of the Receiving and Inspection Process

Documentation and good record keeping are essential to a public agency's ability to deal effectively with contractors whose performance falls below acceptable performance standards. Documentation also provides legal justification for withholding payment until identified problems are corrected.

...the basic functionalities... should be in place so that there is a formal process for reporting delivery discrepancies and non-conformance issues.

The public agency needs to document the receipt of products and the results of the inspection process to support final acceptance or rejection. Receiving and inspection procedures should outline how goods and services are received and inspected and the resolution process for complaints or unsatisfactory deliveries.

In many cases, the receiving and inspection reporting mechanisms have been incorporated into an automated procurement system that links the purchasing, receiving, and payable functions in a database. Regardless of whether the process is automated or paper-intensive, the basic functionalities identified in this section should be in place so that there is a formal process for reporting delivery discrepancies and non-conformance issues.

Receiving and inspection personnel should send copies of receiving and inspection reports, documentation of nonconformance, noncompliance, and other complaints to the Contracting Officer. Many jurisdictions use observation records, standard receiving and inspection reports, contractor complaint forms, nonconformance reports, requests for corrective action, and product information reports for this purpose. These reports can be combined into a single multi-purpose report. Whatever the source of information, the goal of the Contract Administration Team is to tie together all available information to create a comprehensive picture of a contractor's performance. A brief description of several key reports follows.

Observation Record. An observation record is used to document contractor performance on a periodic basis, either through scheduled or non-scheduled visits. Construction, highway repair, technology, and janitorial service contracts are examples of contracts that readily document performance through direct observation.

Receiving Report. This report identifies the item, quantity, and expected delivery time and includes a space for receiving personnel to indicate actual quantities received and note any discrepancies or problems. If problems occur, receiving personnel should notify the Contracting Officer.

Discrepancy Report or Non-Conformance Report. This report is used to document the details of any contractor's action or inaction that does not comply with contractual requirements or describes any item received that does not conform to specification and could lead to a breach of contract. This report is prepared by the field or contract manager (Contract Officer's Representative) and forwarded to the Contracting Officer who, in turn, reviews the nature of the discrepancy based on the contract's specifications or scope of work and brings the discrepancy to the contractor's attention. The Contracting Officer should request that the contractor respond in writing within a specified time. Depending on the contractor's response, the Contracting Officer will decide whether further corrective action should be taken to prevent recurrence of the problem.

Methods for Proper Acceptance, Remedies, or Rejection

Acceptance

The acceptance process is a critical part of contract administration. Acceptance entitles the contractor to payment and limits the rights of the public agency to seek remedies if defects are found at a later date. Section 2-606(1) of the U.C.C. defines acceptance as:

> (1) Acceptance of goods occurs when the buyer:
>   (a) after a reasonable opportunity to inspect the goods, signifies to the seller that the goods are conforming or that he will take or retain them in spite of their nonconformity; or
>   (b) fails to make an effective rejection (subsection (1) of Section 2-602), but such acceptance does not occur until the buyer has had a reasonable opportunity to inspect them; or
>   (c) does any act inconsistent with the seller's ownership; but if such act is wrongful as against the seller it is an acceptance only if ratified by him.

An acceptance clause should be included in the bid documents issued during the solicitation process or, at a minimum, within the contract document executed between the public agency and the contractor. The acceptance clause should contain the following information:

Authority to Accept. The acceptance clause should identify those persons positions and functional titles authorized to accept work for or on behalf of An example is contained in the regulations established by the U.S within FAR 46.502, which states:

Acceptance of supplies is the responsibility of the contracting officer. When the responsibility is assigned to a cognizant contract administration office or to another agency [see 42.201(c)], acceptance by that office or agency is binding on the Government.

Time and Place of Acceptance. Acceptance should occur as promptly as practicable after completion and inspection of the work. The contract should specify if the place of acceptance will be the source where the product was manufactured/produced, the location where the product was shipped, or the destination where the product was delivered or utilized.

Methods of Acceptance. The acceptance clause may specify the exact acceptance method (also known as a formal acceptance clause) or may imply how acceptance is determined. An example of a formal acceptance clause is contained in FAR 46.501 General, which states:

> Acceptance constitutes acknowledgement that the supplies or services conform with applicable contract quality and quantity requirements, except as provided in this subpart and subject to other terms and conditions of the contract. Acceptance may take place before delivery, at time of delivery, or after delivery, depending on the provisions of the terms and conditions of the contract. Supplies or services shall ordinarily not be accepted before completion of the Government's contract quality assurance actions (however, see 46.504). Acceptance shall ordinarily be evidenced by execution of an acceptance certificate on an inspection or receiving report form or commercial shipping document/packing list.

In contrast to a formal acceptance clause, implied acceptance occurs when the public agency does not issue a formal acceptance notice but decides to use the goods, provide payment, or issue a rejection notice that is not sent promptly. If the public agency uses the goods consistent with ownership (e.g., the operation of a snowplow for 60 days), the agency's use implies acceptance, even if the goods are damaged or destroyed while in use by the agency. Final payment for goods and services may also imply acceptance.

Remedies for Defects

UCC Section 2-711(1) specifies the following general remedies for defects discovered prior to acceptance:

> (1) Where the seller fails to make delivery or repudiates or the buyer rightfully rejects or justifiably revokes acceptance then with respect to any goods involved, and with respect to the whole if the breach goes to the whole contract (Section 2-612), the buyer may cancel and whether or not he has done so may in addition to recovering so much of the price as has been paid
> (a) "cover" and have damages under the next section as to all the goods affected whether or not they have been identified to the contract; or

(b) recover damages for non-delivery as provided in this Article (Section 2-713).

(2) Where the seller fails to deliver or repudiates, the buyer may also

(a) if the goods have been identified recover them as provided in this Article (Section 2-502); or

(b) in a proper case obtain specific performance or replevy the goods as provided in this Article (Section 2-716).

(3) On rightful rejection or justifiable revocation of acceptance a buyer has a security interest in goods in his possession or control for any payments made on their price and any expenses reasonably incurred in their inspection, receipt, transportation, care and custody and may hold such goods and resell them in like manner as an aggrieved seller (Section 2-706).

The public agency can consider three options for seeking remedies for defects prior to acceptance.

Require the Contractor to Correct the Defects. A standard inspection clause for the purchase of supplies and construction should include language that addresses correction of defective work by the contractor. The supply contract inspection clause used by the U.S. Federal Government under FAR 52.246-2(f) allows the Federal Government to reject or require correction of the nonconforming supplies. The construction contract inspection clause states that the contractor will "without charge, replace or correct defective work found by the Government not to conform to the contract requirements unless, in the public interest, the Government consents to accept the work with an appropriate adjustment in price."

In all cases where the contractor is formally requested to correct defects, the contractor should submit the proposed corrective measures to the public agency for approval. Typically, the contractor should either offer to correct the defects, offer a price reduction in exchange for acceptance of work, and/or present a case to dispute the facts presented in a rejection notice. Although unusual, the contractor may agree with the notice but offer no solution or may not respond at all.

In response to proposed corrective measures offered by the contractor, the public agency is permitted to extend the contract completion date for a reasonable amount of time to allow the contractor to correct minor defects. If the defects are major and cannot be completed in a reasonable amount of time, the public agency has the right to terminate the contract.

Price Reduction, Acceptance of Minor Nonconformities. The doctrine of substantial completion allows a public agency to accept a product or service with minor nonconformities when correction would cause economic waste. Economic waste occurs when the public agency receives work that substantially complies with the specifications and the cost to replace or repair the defect would be wasteful. The public agency is entitled to receive monetary compensation from the contractor based on a decrease in the value of the work or the amount of savings realized by the contractor due to nonconformities. Accepting a minor nonconformity does not provide relief for correcting similar defects on existing or future contracts. Generally, a minor nonconformance does not adversely affect safety, health, reliability, durability, performance, interchangeability of parts or assemblies, weight (if a contract requirement), appearance (if a contract requirement), or any other fundamental requirement of the product.

Correction of Defects by Public Agency or an Agent. Standard inspection clauses typically allow the public agency or its agent to replace, correct defective work or perform the services, and to charge these costs to the contractor once the contractor is given an opportunity to correct the work and fails to complete the correction within a reasonable amount of time.

Rejection

Rejection is the formal process used by the public agency to officially notify the contractor that the product or service is defective and that it will not be accepted. Remedies may or may not be pursued prior to the official rejection process, although the options are similar. As previously mentioned, it is crucial to determine the conditions for proper rejection and acceptance. If a product is accepted, the public agency's rights of rejection at a later date are very limited. The inspection clause should provide the public agency with the right to issue a rejection notice with or without specific directions for correcting the defective work as well as the right to terminate the contract if the delivery date has passed. If the delivery date has not passed, the contractor must be allowed to correct the defect within the delivery schedule.

If a product or service is rejected, the public agency can pursue any of the following options:

- The public agency can determine that the contractor is not entitled to payment.
- The public agency can pursue corrective action.
- The public agency can pursue an equitable adjustment in price.
- The public agency can determine that there has been contract default and pursue damages.

The rejection process involves the following steps:

- Identify reasons for rejection.
- Acknowledge the limitations to the right to reject.
- Prove defects exist.
- Complete rejection notification procedures.

Identify Reasons for Rejection. Section 2-601 of the UCC states that the public agency, as a buyer, has the right to expect and enforce strict compliance with all contract requirements. The public agency does not have to allow substitutes even if they are superior to the initial requirements. The contractor is not allowed to judge what is acceptable to the public agency. Further, the public agency is not required to demonstrate that deviation from strict compliance will cause it harm. The purpose of strict compliance is to protect the public agency's interest by ensuring that the contractor delivers what was specified by the public agency in its solicitation documents and promised by the contractor through its bid or proposal so that the contractor does not provide an alternate product or service, especially a substitute item that could be less expensive.

Limitations to the Right to Reject. Common law has modified the right of rejection for strict compliance to address the following conditions:

- *Adequate Description and Measurements*. The public agency must provide an adequate description of the requirement and must also have the ability to accurately measure the requirement in order to reject work for strict compliance failure. If a specification is not precisely stated or cannot be accurately measured, the public agency can only reject the work if it is not suitable for its intended purpose.

- *Substantial Completion*. The doctrine of substantial completion limits the public agency's remedies when rejecting work on the basis of strict compliance. Two required elements must exist to meet the test of substantial completion: forfeiture and economic waste. Economic waste occurs when the public agency receives work that substantially complies with the specifications and the cost to replace or repair the defect is wasteful. The public agency is entitled to receive monetary compensation from the contractor based on the decrease in value of the work or the amount of savings realized by the contractor.

The purpose of strict compliance is to protect the public agency's interest...

- *Correctable Defects*. Major defects are the basis for strict compliance rejection and contract termination. If a defect is easily correctable, the public agency cannot terminate the contract based on strict compliance. If the work is rejected for failure to strictly comply, the contractor must prove the defect may be correctable.

- *Previous Action*. Previous acceptance of nonconforming work does not relieve the contractor of strict compliance if the public agency was unaware of the nonconformance. If the contractor can demonstrate that the public agency previously accepted the work fully aware of the nonconformance, the contractor can successfully demonstrate that the public agency waived its right to strict compliance.

Prove Defects Exist. The public agency must prove that defects exist and contract requirements have not been met by demonstrating that the contract contained an adequate description of the requirement and that the requirement can be and was accurately measured. The results of any inspection and testing must be submitted to the contractor for review. It is the contractor's responsibility to prove that the specifications were inadequate or the testing was not conducted properly.

Rejection Notification Procedure. The Notice of Rejection must be sent to the contractor in a timely manner and contain the reasons for rejection and the time period for the contractor's reply. A rejection notice does not extend the delivery period. It is acceptable to discuss the rejection with the contractor before issuing any written notification. This discussion may determine whether the contractor has additional information regarding the deliverable or was directed to make a change in the contract requirements.

The time period for issuing a Notice of Rejection depends on the type of product or service, the complexity of the inspection, and the effect of a delay on the contractor. The notification is not timely if its delay prevents the contractor from reworking or repairing the defective item or causes the contractor additional work or expense. The Notice of Rejection must include the reasons for rejection. If the public agency provides the wrong reasons, the contractor may be entitled to compensation for the extra work done. The contractor has the right to correct the defects within a reasonable amount of time. The amount of time depends on the type of product or service, the complexity of the inspection, and the effect of a delay on the public agency.

Post Acceptance Rights

Acceptance substantially limits the public agency's ability to reject goods or services if a defect is found at a later date. In fact, one of the following conditions must exist for the public agency to seek a remedy after an item or service has been accepted:

- Latent Defects
- Warranties
- Fraud
- Gross Mistakes amounting to Fraud

Latent Defects

Latent defects exist at the time of acceptance, but could not have been discovered through normal and reasonable inspection procedures. An example of a latent defect is a standard, off-the-shelf personal computer with a defective hard drive. During initial inspection, it is determined that all of the components have shipped and appear to be undamaged. When the unit is set up for use, it is determined that the hard drive is defective. This type of defect cannot be expected to be discovered during normal inspection procedures. The public agency has the responsibility for proving a defect was latent through one of the following conditions.

Determining that the Defect was Not Known During Initial Inspection. If the public agency is aware of the defect at the time of acceptance, the defect is patent, and the public agency is not entitled to relief.

Nature of Inspection. If the item is critical to the contract and/or if a detailed or performance specification was provided to all bidders during the solicitation process, it is likely that the public agency will be required to test for conformance to these specifications prior to acceptance. This increases the burden of proof on the public agency to demonstrate why the defect was not discovered prior to acceptance.

Ease of Inspection. A defect may be latent if operating the item for an extended period of time is the primary means for discovering the defect. This would include defects that were undetected during a shorter operational trial as well as equipment containing sealed subcomponents that have to be destroyed or maximized in order to inspect the equipment.

Reliance on Contractor Testing. Previous experience, past performance, and contractor representations may determine the reasonableness of the amount of public agency testing required. If the contractor is experienced and the work is routine, less testing is reasonable. On the other hand, if the contractor is not experienced, it is reasonable to expect that more testing would be required as a condition for acceptance.

Fraud

All of the following factors must be present in order for the public agency to revoke acceptance based on fraud:

- Misrepresentation of fact, actual or implied, or the concealment of a material fact
- Knowledge of falsity or reckless or wanton disregard of the facts
- Intention to mislead the public agency into relying on the misrepresentations
- Injury suffered by the public agency.

Gross Mistake amounting to Fraud

This is a major mistake made by the contractor so serious and uncalled for as not to be reasonably expected or justifiable. The requirements to prove gross mistake are the same as fraud with the exception of proving there was intent to mislead.

Warranties

Warranty clauses provide the public agency a remedy for latent or patent defects discovered after acceptance. The following factors should be considered when making a decision to include a warranty clause:

- increased costs associated with the warranty clause
- the ability of the public agency to administer and enforce the warranty

- the type of supply or service
- normal trade practices for this type of supply or service
- possibility of reduced quality assurance prior to acceptance and greater reliance on discovery of defects after acceptance.

There are two types of warranties: express and implied.

Express Warranty. An express warranty is an explicit, written promise by the contractor to provide a specified level of quality, condition, description, or performance of a good or service. Defects not specifically stated in a warranty clause are excluded from consideration. Warranty clauses should be broad. The warranty clause used by the Federal Government for supplies of a non-complex nature (FAR 52.246-17[b1i]) states:

> (1) Notwithstanding inspection and acceptance by the Government of supplies furnished under this contract, or any conditions of this contract concerning the conclusiveness thereof, the Contractor warrants (Contracting Officer shall state the specific period of time after delivery, or the specified event whose occurrence will terminate the warranty period; e.g., the number of miles or hours of use, or combinations of any applicable events or periods of time)
> (i) All supplies furnished under this contract will be free from defects in material or workmanship and will conform with all requirements of this contract.

The warranty clause for construction contracts (FAR 52.246-21[a]) states: "Work performed under this contract conforms to the contract requirements and is free of any defects in equipment, material, or design furnished, or workmanship performed by the Contractor or any sub-Contractor or Contractor at any tier."

Implied Warranties. Implied warranties are obligations of the contractor that have not been assumed in expressed language. The UCC provides additional details on implied warranties of merchantability and implied warranties for fitness for particular purposes. These implied warranties may be used in supply contracts that do not contain a standard inspection clause that defines acceptance. On the other hand, if the public agency accepts the supplies after conducting a physical inspection and subsequently discovers a patent defect, the right to implied warranty is lost.

Under the **implied warranty of merchantability**, the UCC requires that the goods sold by the contractor be reasonably fit for the normal purpose that they are made for and are of fair and average quality. Specifically, UCC 2-314 states the minimum requirements for merchantability as:

> (a) pass without objection in the trade under the contract description, and
> (b) in the case of fungible goods, be of fair average quality with the description, and
> (c) be fit for the ordinary purposes for which the goods are used, and

(d) run, within variations permitted by the agreement, of even kind, quality and quantity within each unit and among all units involved, and

(e) be adequately contained, packaged, and labeled as the agreement may require, and

(f) conform to the promises or affirmations of fact made on the container or label, if any.

Under the **implied warranty of fitness for a particular purpose**, Section 2-315 of the UCC specifically states:

> Where the seller at the time of contracting has reason to know any particular purpose for which the goods are required, and that the buyer is relying on the seller's skill or judgement to select or furnish suitable goods, there is unless excluded or modified under the next section, an implied warranty that the goods shall be fit for such purpose.

Notice and Burden of Proof. The public agency has the responsibility to notify a contractor that a warranty has been breached and has the responsibility of proving the breach. This notification is similar to that given for rejecting items during the inspection process.

Remedies for Breach of Warranty. If specific remedies are stated in a warranty clause, the public agency is limited to those remedies and cannot impose stricter remedies. The remedies for breach of a standard warranty clause are identical to remedies for work rejected under the inspection and acceptance clause:

Require the Contractor to Correct the Defects. The public agency can require the contractor to correct the defects at the contractor's cost.

Price Reduction (acceptance of minor non-conformities). The public agency can negotiate a price reduction and accept the work if the conformities are minor.

Correction of Defects by Public Agency or another Contractor. The public agency can correct the defects or use another contractor to correct the defects. The public agency has the right to collect, from the initial contractor, any differences between the cost to correct the defect and the contracted price.

After the expiration of the warranty period, the public agency continues to have rights and remedies under the inspection clause relating to latent defects, fraud, and gross mistakes, because these rights are not limited to a specific time period.

Inspection and Acceptance Considerations

- What are the key performance characteristics for/of the deliverables? Alternatively, what are the performance metrics, i.e. the post-acceptance performance that is desired or required per the contract deliverables? How are latent defect issues resolved?

- If a performance-based procurement approach has been used, what are the most efficient and effective pre-acceptance inspection criteria for buyer review and approval? (A Performance-Based Guide is available at www.acquisition.gov/comp/seven_steps/home.html)

- What did market research reveal as best practices for inspection, ISO certification etc. for similar or same services or supplies? What are the commercially accepted standards for inspection and acceptance and have they been incorporated into the contract?

- What level of oversight is necessary during contract performance? When and how will inspection/acceptance criteria contained in the contract be utilized during contract performance?

- What are the post-acceptance quality or performance metrics? How will they be monitored to ensure that stated levels of performance are met?
  - Mean-Time-Between-Failures (MTBF)?
  - Number of user complaints over a set period of time?
  - Number of defects?
  - Other?

- How are post-acceptance performance metrics described in the contract vis a vis the inspection and acceptance clause? There must be a link between the requirements of the work statement and the inspection and acceptance provisions of the contract.

References

Cibinic, J., Jr., & Nash, R. C., Jr. (1995). *Administration of government contracts* (3rd ed.). Washington, DC: The George Washington University.

Federal Acquisition Regulations Web Site, www.arnet.gov/far/loadmainre.html.

Thai, K. V., Ph.D. (2007). *Introduction to public procurement. (2nd ed.).* Herndon, VA: NIGP.

Chapter 8

Contract Modifications

Introduction

With rare exception, all contracts will undergo modification. The need for modifications can be predicted in some instances; and, in others, the need to modify a contract may be emergent. Modifications can alter routine administrative matters within the contract, correct minor errors or make substantive changes to the terms of agreement by the parties. Modifications must be well thought out, written, and considered in terms of immediate and long-term consequences. This chapter will focus on contract modifications in the following areas:

- Classifying types of modifications
- Constructive changes
- Request for Equitable Adjustment (REA)
- Pricing and negotiation of modifications.

Classifying Types of Modifications

Contract modifications are issued as either bilateral or unilateral, so it is important to understand the parameters of both types.

Bilateral Modifications

Bilateral modifications to the contract require the approval of both parties in signatory form. In most cases, the contract modification will state that it is to be executed by both parties to be binding. Bilateral modifications are typically prepared by the public agency's Contracting Officer and forwarded to the contractor for review and approval. Once the contractor has executed the modification, it is executed on behalf of the public agency.

Bilateral modifications are often related to some alteration of one or more substantive terms of the contract. Because substantive changes can cause significant changes to the rights and obligations of one or both parties, bilateral execution serves as a protection mechanism so that both parties are fully aware of the nature of the changes. Doing so permits the parties to assess the implications of the modifications.

For example, a change that alters the electronic format of deliverables required under the contract may seem harmless at first glance. However, consider the dilemma of a contractor who lacks the software program and training necessary to comply with the new format requirements. A modification under these circumstances might require an adjustment in contract price. Alternatively, the proposed new electronic format may have been recommended by the contractor because it is available and in use. In such cases, it would seem that no adjustment in contract price would be warranted. In all circumstances, the modification should contain clear and complete language delineating the affect of the modification on the price and/or delivery schedule (or other contractual requirements). Such a statement binds the rights of the parties to seek compensation at some later date. For example, if the parties agree that the modification does not affect price, delivery, or other contractual requirements, the modification could state: As a result of this modification, there is no change to contract price, delivery, or other terms and conditions. Including such language helps to avoid future claims for recovery.

Unilateral Modifications

Unilateral modification can occur for two reasons: (1) the right to unilaterally modify the contract has been given to the public agency in the contract itself or (2) the modification is for a minor purpose. Careful attention to the use of unilateral modification authority must be exercised. An example of a unilateral modification is the public agency's right to make a change to the contract pursuant to the changes clause of a contract. Unilateral modifications only require execution by the public agency's Contracting Officer. In other words, the contractor is not required to sign the modification for it to have its full force and effect.

Contracts can contain prescribed terms and conditions that permit unilateral modification of the contract. For example, in the basic contract, the parties may have agreed to the public agency's right to order additional quantities or supplies within 90 days of contract execution. Such language provides the public agency with the right to simply modify the contract and order the additional quantities within the stated boundaries (*within ninety days . . .*). In this case, the public agency is within its contractual rights to order additional quantities given compliance with the "ground rules" established by the parties in the contract. In exchange for this right, the contractor obtains additional work. If, however, the public agency orders the additional quantities outside of the ordering period, the unilateral modification is a breach of the contract and the additional order is unenforceable. As a practical matter, however, given the contractor's ability to meet the additional ordering requirements and the opportunity to make a profit, it seems unlikely that the contractor would turn away an order, even if it exceeded the scope of its terms. The lesson is a simple one: A unilateral modification must be within the rights of the public agency to issue.

The second type of unilateral modification is issued to correct minor clerical errors or administrative matters that are not related to price, delivery, or other terms and conditions. The Contracting Officer is cautioned to carefully examine the circumstances surrounding the intent to issue such a unilateral modification to determine if it meets the test. If doubt exists as to whether or not the modification should be executed unilaterally, the Contracting Officer should discuss the content of the modification with the contractor and/or issue the modification bilaterally.

Change Order Authority

One of the far-reaching rights contained in many public agency contracts is the right to unilaterally change the contract. The right, commonly known as the "changes authority," gives the public agency the right to make certain changes to the contract without express consent of the contractor. As stated above, this authority represents a unilateral modification. Note that, in many cases, the parties negotiate the change prior to commencement of the changed work and execute a bilateral modification.

The language of the change clause establishes the boundaries of contract modifications that can be made. For example, supply contracts typically limit the right to make changes to (1) method of delivery, (2) place of delivery, and (3) work statements (specifications).

Constructive Changes

Definition and Parameters

Constructive changes are any actions or inactions on the part of the public agency that have not been made through formal change order authority but have caused the contractor to perform additional work that is outside the scope of the existing contract. Constructive changes pose difficult and unique challenges for Contracting Officers, because oftentimes the change is not viewed as such by the public agency. Typical constructive change actions occur when direction is given (or is perceived to have been given) by someone within the public agency who lacks the authority to order the change. In many circumstances, the public agency's view may be that the change constituted a valid change or, perhaps, work that could not be considered a change.

In constructive change disagreements, if the contractor prevails, the public agency is considered to have breached the contract and the contractor is entitled to compensation for additional costs incurred when performing the changed work. Alternatively, if the public agency prevails (i.e., the work does not meet the test of a change), the contractor is entitled to no additional compensation.

Compensation can be in the form of additional time, money, or both; however, for compensation to be recognized, entitlement must be proven. Simply incurring additional costs does not in itself constitute a change, nor does the mere establishment of entitlement automatically give the contractor the right to compensation. In other words, a change may have occurred, but the contractor incurred no additional costs in complying with the work as changed. For the public agency to be liable, the contractor must establish the following:

- The work "ordered" was the act of a public agency employee with authority.

- The additional work exceeded the scope of the existing contract.

- Timely notice is provided to the public agency about the order. This third element will vary depending on the specific contractual language. (Note: Some contracts specifically state that the contractor must notify the public agency within a specific number of days from which it received an "order" to do something that it believes constitutes a change.)

Types of Constructive Changes

Constructive changes occur for any number of reasons but can be grouped into specific categories.

Contract Interpretation. A constructive change can occur when the public agency interprets the contract during performance of the work in a manner that is more expensive than the interpretation upon which the contractor relied. Contract interpretation must address the meaning of the contract language when the parties to the contract differ and must also determine who should bear the risk of misinterpretation. The responsibility to ensure that the contract is explicit is born by the drafter. This is known as the "doctrine of contra proferentum."

Interference. Public agency interference during performance of the work can result in a constructive change. An example of interference would be in process inspections that negatively impact the operation of a production line. Consider the dilemma of the Food and Drug Administration inspector who must inspect poultry processing operations at a poultry plant without disrupting the production line.

Failure to Cooperate. Failure to cooperate can also cause a constructive change. The actions or inactions of public agency representatives with contractual authority of some kind can fail to cooperate in a manner that harms the contractor. For example, failure to inspect at a stated place, time, and date would be considered a constructive change.

Nondisclosure of Important Information. If the public agency has information that is vital to the contractor's successful performance and it fails to disclose such information, a constructive change will be held to have occurred. Three elements are commonly recognized for this argument to prevail:

- The public agency has possession of the information.

- The contractor is unable to obtain the information through normal channels.

- The public agency knows (implied or actual knowledge) that the contractor does not have the information.

Work Acceleration. If the contractor is ordered to accelerate work in a manner that causes him to incur additional costs, a constructive change will be held to have occurred. Constructive acceleration can also occur when the public agency's Contracting Officer fails to recognize an excusable delay, which may prevent the contractor from performing in accordance with the contractual schedule.

Defective or Ambiguous Specification or Work Statement. As the drafter of the contract (and work statement), the public agency is held responsible for the quality of that work product. Defects or ambiguities that are uncovered during performance of the work are construed against the drafter. The public agency may prevail with the counter-argument that the contractor "should have known." Consider the construction contractor who successfully wins the bid to construct a building and completes all plumbing work according to the drawings supplied by the public agency. Unfortunately, these drawings fail to include plumbing requirements for the toilets. In this particular case, the contractor argued defective specifications and attempted to hold the public agency accountable for the specification. The court, however, saw things differently, stating that the contractor should have known that regardless of the drawings, toilets require plumbing.

Obligation to Proceed

Generally speaking, the contractor has an obligation to proceed while any disagreement or dispute regarding the validity of a change is being resolved. However, as a practical matter, if a contractor refuses to perform the changed work and is found to prevail in the argument, they suffer no harm. If, however, they refuse to perform and do not prevail in the argument, they will be considered in breach of contract, which can result in contract termination. In some contracts, specific contractual language states that the contractor must continue working under the revision while the matter is being resolved.

Change Order Accounting

It is useful to include a change order accounting clause in all contracts. Such a clause requires the contractor to segregate the costs associated with the changed work in order that such specific costs can be accumulated and negotiated. Change order accounting is easily accomplished through most software programs. The separation of costs associated with the changed work allows the public agency's Contracting Officer to examine those costs separately. Conversely, the inability to separate the costs of changed work makes cost analysis difficult.

Request for Equitable Adjustment (REA)

C hanged work, either directed by formal contract modification or through constructive change, entitles the contractor to seek an equitable adjustment. Seeking such an adjustment does not automatically entitle the contractor to more money and/or time. Requests for such relief must be proven because a change may in fact have occurred but may have not resulted in increased cost or schedule slippage.

Entitlement is the first step whereby the contractor proves that he is entitled to an equitable adjustment. This step may be easier to prove than the second step—quantum. Quantum is the sum of adjustment to which the contractor is entitled. Quantum may be time, money, or both. Recognize that while a contractor may be able to prove entitlement, he may have difficulty proving the quantum. Quantum will always be subject to negotiation.

A contract clause may contain a provision for an equitable adjustment if an event specified in the contract occurs that increases or decreases the contractor's cost of performing the contract. A Request for Equitable Adjustment (REA) is a price adjustment requested by the contractor or the public agency to cover this type of claim that may have otherwise have been considered damages for breach of contract.

Conditions under which an REA will be Considered

The contract clause must contain language specifying the conditions under which an REA will be considered. For example, the U.S. Federal Government's FAR 52.212.12, Suspension of Work states: "An adjustment shall be made for any increase in the cost of performance of this contract (excluding profit) necessarily caused by such unreasonable suspension, delay or interruption, and the contract modified in writing accordingly."

If·' contract contains an equitable adjustment clause, the contractor may not seek damages ·ach of contract for the conditions discussed below.

Burden of Proof

The pricing adjustment must be a direct result of an event that causes the contractor to perform differently from the original contract and create a change in costs proven to be directly related to that event. The party claiming the benefit of the adjustment has the burden of convincing the other party that a price adjustment is necessary and for establishing the amount of the adjustment. The public agency has the burden of proving how much the price should be adjusted downward if work has been deleted and the contractor has the burden of proving how much costs have increased.

Methods to measure the amount of a Price Adjustment

Once both parties have agreed to consider an REA, the equitable pricing adjustment will have to be established. Most pricing adjustments are settled through negotiation. The price adjustment will be a result of one of the following actions caused by the event that triggered the REA:

Actions that Add Work. The method generally used to determine the equitable pricing adjustment for actions adding work is to calculate the costs reasonably incurred by the contractor. It is not generally acceptable to use the market value or another contractor's cost to determine the equitable pricing adjustment for actions that add work.

Actions that Delete Work. The amount of the deduction is determined by calculating the net savings to the contractor for the work deleted. The deleted work is calculated at the same price the Contractor would have paid if the work had not been deleted. It is not calculated as the amount included in the original cost estimate.

Deletion of work in construction subcontracts provides an example. The contractor's original price estimate for plumbing work may not have provided adequate pricing detail for every subsystem. When a portion of the work is deleted, the subcontractor's actual price for the deleted work may be different from the original estimate. Exceptions are allowed in the following cases:

- When minor items are deleted from a contract and the bid price can be used as a basis for determining the amount of the deduction; and

- When the original cost estimate provides the best proof of cost of the deleted work or when both parties agree in advance that the unit price will be used to determine pricing deductions.

The public agency is entitled to a deduction for deleted work even if the Contractor did not include the work or a price for the work in the cost estimate.

Actions that Delete One Item and Substitute Another Item. To determine the net equitable pricing adjustment for actions that delete one item and substitute another item, the amount of the deduction for the deleted item is calculated using the equitable pricing adjustment method for work deleted. The amount of the increase in costs for the substituted item is calculated using the equitable pricing adjustment method for additional work. The two adjustments are compared, and the net result is the equitable pricing.

Reasonably Incurred Costs

Reasonably incurred costs are "the difference between what it would have reasonably cost to perform the work as originally required and what it would reasonably cost to perform the work as changed" (*Modern Foods, Inc.*, ABSCA 2090, 57-1 BCA paragraph 1229; *Jack Picoult*, VACAB 1221, 78-1 BCA paragraph 13,024). The following factors are considered to determine the change in any reasonably incurred costs.

Allowable Costs. To qualify as an allowable cost, the cost must be for work performed within the terms of the contract the public agency has agreed to reimburse, and the costs must be reasonable. A cost is reasonable if it does not exceed what a reasonable person would incur in the operation of a competitive business. The cost of preparing an REA is an allowable cost under certain conditions.

Subcontractor Costs. If a change affects a subcontractor's costs, the contractor will negotiate an equitable adjustment with the subcontractor and include this amount with the REA.

Impact and Delay. Under this scenario, the REA is based on the contractor's claim that the delay is having a direct impact on increasing costs because of idleness. An REA for impact and delays provides compensation to the contractor for performing unneeded work, performing inefficiently, stoppage of work, performing work during different hours, or changing the work process. Delays resulting from defective specifications are entitled to an REA. The contractor is also entitled to impact and delay the REA as a result of changed site or work conditions that could not be reasonably foreseen. Reasonable delays preceding a change order are not entitled to an REA.

Reasonably incurred costs are "the difference between what it would have reasonably cost to perform the work as originally required and what it would reasonably cost to perform the work as changed."

Changes in Material and Labor Costs. If the REA is due to a delay caused by a public agency, increases in material and labor costs that have been incurred are allowable.

Overhead and Profit. An REA for any changes in overhead or profit must be a result of costs that were directly increased or decreased as a result of the change. If an REA for overhead and profit is approved, the amount of the increase will usually be determined by using the *usual and customary* percentages for that industry.

Methods of determining Costs for the Amount of Adjustment

As indicated earlier with regard to contract modification provisions, the following methods are similarly used to prove that the costs of an adjustment are reasonable.

Actual Cost Data. The desired method for determining the amount of pricing adjustment is the submittal of actual costs for the additional work by the contractor. The public agency has the right to audit these costs or accounting records.

Estimates. Estimates are frequently used to determine the cost of deleted work. Estimates may be used if actual costs for additional work do not exist. When determining the amount of change in profit, the contractor is entitled to reasonable and customary allowance for profit. The public agency has the right to determine if the costs are reasonable.

Jury Verdict. The jury verdict is used to determine equitable pricing when there is enough evidence to make a reasonable determination of equitable pricing but there is conflicting factual evidence and the parties cannot agree on which set of facts to use. Under this scenario, both parties rely on the evaluation and recommendation of a "jury" ("the Board or Court acting as a jury") of independent experts who evaluate the work and assign some monetary value to determine equitable pricing. Generally, in rendering a jury verdict, only a determination of the amount is made. No justification or explanation is necessarily provided.

Pricing and Negotiation of Modifications

Whether the subject of changed work or not, contract modifications may result in adjustments to price, schedule, or both. With regard to scheduling, the Contracting Officer must carefully examine the causes of schedule slippage to ensure that scheduling renegotiation is proper and not caused by the failure of the contractor but caused by the public agency's modification to the contract. A careful analysis of the causes of schedule and cost increases is necessary to ensure that the parties "remain whole," i.e., as they were at the time the contract was executed. The following are three commonly recognized methods that identify and negotiate the costs associated with a contract modification, e.g., change to the contract.

Total Cost Method

The total cost method is the least preferred method of negotiating costs. It is used when the contractor is unable or not required by the contract to segregate the costs associated with the modification. The total cost method uses the total cost of the work as originally contained in the contract and the total cost of the contract work, including the change to develop the difference between the two. That difference is used as the basis for identifying the value of the changed work. Using this method poses special challenges for the Contracting Off because it fails to recognize other factors that may have contributed to the new total cost of the work as changed. Thus, cost overruns not related to the changed work will be included in the cost of the total work as changed.

Jury Verdict Approach

When the parties cannot reach agreement on the value of the modified work, the jury verdict approach can be used. It relies on the evaluation and recommendation of a "jury" of independent experts who evaluate the work and assign some monetary value to the work as modified.

Actual Cost

The actual cost method is the preferred method of negotiating the value of modified/changed work. It requires the contractor to have in place an accounting system that segregates the costs associated with the changed work. In this manner, the parties are able to examine those costs without the burden of isolating those costs from the total cost pools. The actual cost of the work, as modified, is recorded in separate accounts and is easily examined. The actual cost of the modified work forms the basis for the contractor's request for equitable adjustment. Contracting Officers are reminded that it should not be presumed that actual costs incurred are reasonable; rather, costs incurred should be examined for reasonableness, allow ability and allocability, regardless of the fact that the cost has been incurred.

Contract modifications are common during contract performance and can pose unique challenges for the most seasoned Contracting Officer. Close communication with the contractor and other members of the public agency Contract Administration Team will help to ensure that modifications are managed and written in a manner that is clear and understandable to all affected parties. Ongoing dialogue and communication among the Contract Administration Team members will help to facilitate the modification process and permit the parties to anticipate and be proactive rather than reactive to modifications and changes. Managing modifications and changes through ongoing communications among all team members facilitates the contract administration process.

References

Cibinic, J., Jr., & Nash, R. C., Jr. (1995). *Administration of government contracts* (3rd ed.). Washington, DC: The George Washington University.

Federal Acquisition Regulations Web Site, www.arnet.gov/far/loadmainre.html.

Worthington, M. M., & Goldsman, L. P. (1998). *Contracting with the Federal Government* (4th ed.). New York: John Wiley and Sons.

Chapter 9

Software Management: The Contractual Perspective and Data Deliverables during a Contract

Overview

This section provides a more focused examination of contract administration considerations for software contracts. It will also focus on rights regarding technical data delivered under contracts.

It's one of the oldest jokes in the Internet, endlessly forwarded from email box to email box: A software mogul - usually Bill Gates, but sometimes another - makes a speech. "If the automobile industry had developed like the software industry", the mogul proclaims," we would all be driving $25 cars that get 1,000 miles to the gallon." To which an automobile executive retorts, "yeah, and if cars were like software, they would crash twice a day for no reason, and when you called for service, they'd tell you to reinstall the engine" (Mann, Technology Review, July/August 2002).

Software contract administration can be a formidable task. At one end of the software continuum is commercial software; at the other is software specifically developed to meet specific contract requirements. Commercial software is generally acquired under license and should be acquired with the same rights offered to other commercial buyers. Contract administrators are challenged to ensure that the rights normally conveyed with commercial software are adhered to.

To appreciate the uniqueness of software contract administration, this chapter introduces the contract administrator to terminology, statutes and treaties that govern software, types of software programs, rights of the parties, issues related to management of the software contract and remedies available to the parties. The context is commercial type of software. A detailed discussion of custom developed software would require a text well in excess of the boundaries of this work.

Every contract is different! Contract administrators must have a complete understanding of the contractual language and its enforceability, from a legal and a practical perspective, so that software users can be educated regarding the rights and limitations of use and an effective software management plan can be developed and enforced.

The following is a practical list of key considerations for contract administrators. As a starting point, it is important for buyers to remember the following basic tenets that govern software contracts:

- Quality is the responsibility of the supplier. During contract administration, the buyer must ensure that software "outcome" meets the requirements of the contract.

- Standards provide the verification process through which the supplier (and sometimes the buyer) verifies the quality of the software. During contract administration, the buyer must hold the contractor accountable to the stated standards contained in the contract (and in the contractor's proposal, if that proposal has been incorporated into the contract).

- Metrics are the data which are measured during performance to ensure that the quality meets the stated standard. During contract administration, the buyer must ensure that the key performance parameters of the software are being met at the threshold stated in the contract. The difficulty with software lies in:

  - The interrelationship among different operating systems and software programs may impact the performance of the single software package.
  - Problems encountered must be repeatable and documented so that the contractor can "recreate" the problem the buyer experienced.

Quality is built into software and remains throughout the entire life cycle of the software product. Standards and metrics are often described as the "keystones" of quality. So, to take one step backward from contract administration, selection of a software supplier (or a software program) must consider the extent to which the supplier (or developer) has a foundation of quality based upon the following seven criteria:

1. **Measurements** capture software metrics through testing.

2. **Analysis of the measurements** provides the current state of the process, and along with the known previous states, also provides existing trends.

3. **Configuration control maintains** the documented state of the system at any given time and is directly related to measurements.

4. **Review processes** allow the current state and its trends to be assessed. Developers conduct a risk analysis. If the process is out of compliance with the specifications, developers apply change management techniques through feedback mechanisms. (Note: these feedback mechanisms may be internal quality control, beta testing, or customer feedback on software "glitches").

5. **Compliance** is often manifested through a Capability Maturity Model (CMM) certification.

6. **Security mechanisms** by which the integrity of the software is protected (often linked to CMM certification).

7. **Training** to the extent that customers need to understand application and interrelationships among various software programs.

"You can't just punch in 'let there be light' without writing the code underlying the user interface functions."

Axioms of Software Management: A Primer

In order for contract administrators to do an effective job of managing software contracts, it is important to understand the axioms of software management.

It is a fact that the complexity of software grows during the maintenance phase unless specifically addressed and actions are taken to mitigate this fate. This is partly due to the fact that the size of software typically increases with age along with an accompanying decrease in maintainability.

Software will deteriorate with age. Deterioration of software comes from changes in the software environment (i.e. hardware and software operating systems) as well as from the organizational environment (end user and business processes change).

The CMM model draws upon best practices for development of large software projects; thus buyers need to understand the maturity of the software solutions they are seeking. This model is briefly described under the Terminology section below. (Contract administrators should be cognizant of the CMM level of their suppliers.)

Terminology

In order to further understand the complexities of software contract administration, clear definition of commonly used terms follows:

Data: Recorded information, including computer software. It may come in various forms, paper, electronic etc.

Form, Fit, Function Data: Within the context of software, data identifying source, functional characteristics, and performance requirements. The term generally is defined as excluding source code, algorithm, process, formulae and flow charts of software.

Computer Software: Computer programs and ancillary materials such as human readable instructional listings, flow charts and related instructional material (e.g. maintenance and operating manuals). Computer software can be categorized as commercial software and non-commercial software:

1. *Commercial Software*: Computer software which is generally used for other than "government" purposes and is sold, licensed, or leased in significant quantities to the general public and established market or catalog prices (Federal Acquisition Regulations, 2007). Commercial software is generally developed at expense to the developer and limited rights, as set forth in the licensing agreement, convey.

2. *Non-Commercial Software*: Computer software which is specifically developed to meet performance or process needs as described by the buyer and enforceable under the contract. Non-commercial software is generally developed exclusively for the buyer using public funds; unlimited rights generally convey.

Computer software programs are generally classified into two basic types:

1. *System Programs* which include compilers, the operating systems, the file management systems etc. System programs are produced by computer manufacturers and are generally included with the computer (hardware). Vendors may also sell system software packages.

2. *Application Programs* that provide the user specific results (e.g. payroll, word processing, calculations etc.).

Limited Rights: Data rights of the buyer as specifically set forth in the contract. Limited rights must be described in the bidding documents. It may provide the right of the buyer to use, modify, reproduce, release, perform, display or disclose software data, in whole or in part. The contract must be specific on the extent to which limited rights are conveyed upon the buyer. Contract administrators must develop a contract administration plan that ensures that all software users under the extent of limitations in use. For example, limited rights may be conveyed which allow the user to make emergency repair or make a certain number of copies. Generally, limited rights enable the supplier to protect qualifying restricted computer software by withholding such data from delivery and delivering instead, form, fit and function data.

Restricted Computer Software: Computer software developed at private expense and that is a trade secret (see definition below). It includes published copyrighted computer software, including minor modifications of such software. A sample contract provision for restricted rights software is provided in Appendix B.

Unlimited Rights: Rights of the buyer to use, disclose, reproduce, prepare derivative works, distribute copies to the public and display publicly, in any manner and for any purpose, and to have others or permit others to do so.

Unlimited rights to commercially developed software are extremely rare and administrators are cautioned against any actions or inactions which might result in treatment of commercial software in an "unlimited rights" manner.

Capability Maturity Model (CMM): Developed by the Carnegie Mellon Institute, Software Engineering Institute, CMM represents a series of steps through which software developers and maintainers proceed toward institutionalizing the measures and procedures they use. The CMM recommends:

- documenting the way work is performed
- measuring its performance
- using data for controlling its performance
- planning based upon historical performance
- training people.

The CMM is structured into five maturity levels, which are briefly described as follows:

1. Initial: Software process is characterized as ad hoc, and occasionally even chaotic. Few processes are defined, and success depends on individual effort and heroics.

2. Repeatable: Basic project management processes are established to track cost, schedule and functionality. The necessary process discipline is in place to repeat earlier successes on projects with similar applications.

3. Defined: The software process for both management and engineering activities is documented, standardized, and integrated into a standard software process for the organization. All projects use an approved, tailored version of the organization's standard software process for developing and maintaining software.

4. Managed: Detailed measures of the software process and product quality are collected. Both the software process and products are quantitatively understood and controlled.

5. Optimizing: Continuous process improvement is enabled by quantitative feedback from the process and from piloting innovative ideas and technologies.

(Paulk, et.al, 2005)

Note: For more information on CMM, see www.sei.cmu.edu/cmm)

Contract Licenses/Statutes/Treaties that Govern Software

Contracts

The specific language of contracts is the primary mechanism with which software rights are protected. Leases provide for the delivery of software program(s) for use in accordance with a "Rights in Software" provision of the contract. The most common form of contract used today for protecting software is perhaps "shrink-wrap" or "click on" licenses. Such mechanisms prompt some type of consent by the user prior to installing or using the software program. In "shrink-wrap", by opening the package, the user is consenting to the licensing rights stated therein. "Click-on" licensing requires the user to check "I agree" before the software can be downloaded and installed. Contract administrators must ensure that all users understand the limitations set forth in such licensing as if (and this is often the case) that end users do not read the terms of the license but rather simply check the "I Agree" box.

1976 Copyright Act

The 1976 Copyright Act expanded copyright to computer programs. It defined computer programs as a set of statements or instructions to be used directly or indirectly in a computer in order to bring about a certain result. For purposes of this text, the act clearly covers software, i.e. computer programs making violation of express rights contained in the contract subject to the statute.

Copyright protection has been upheld for:

- source code and object code
- microcode
- systems software and applications software
- data on a hard drive, floppy disc, CD Rom
- visual output of a computer program.

(Rawicz & Nash, 2001)

Uniform Computer Information Transactions Act (UCITA)

The UCITA, 1999, is a uniform act which seeks to create an article for the Uniform Commercial Code that covers licensing. The UCITA has not been adopted by all states. Its provisions are characterized as "default" provisions that can be made applicable to a transaction if the buyer and seller have not otherwise provided for in the contract. The UCITA defines computer information transactions as "an agreement or the performance of it to create, modify, transfer or license computer information. It further defines "computer information" as information in electronic form which is obtained from or through the use of a computer or which is in a form capable of being processed by a computer. The term also includes a copy of the information and any documentation or packaging associated with the copy.

Contract administrators should review contracts to ensure that licensing rights are clearly defined and understood by the parties. By doing so, reliance on the UCITA may be avoided.

Digital Millennium Copyright Act of 1998

This statute (PL 105-304) makes it a crime to circumvent anti-piracy measures built into most commercial software. Specifically it:

- Outlaws the manufacture, sale, or distribution of code-cracking devices used to illegally copy software

- Does permit the cracking of copyright protection devices, however, to conduct encryption research, assess product interoperability, and test computer security systems

- Provides exemptions from anti-circumvention provisions for nonprofit libraries, archives, and educational institutions under certain circumstances

- In general, limits Internet service providers from copyright infringement liability for simply transmitting information over the Internet. Service providers, however, are expected to remove material from users' web sites that appears to constitute copyright infringement

- Limits liability of nonprofit institutions of higher education (when they serve as online service providers and under certain circumstances) for copyright infringement by faculty members or graduate students

- Requires that "webcasters" pay licensing fees to record companies

- Requires that the Register of Copyrights, after consultation with relevant parties, submit to Congress recommendations regarding how to promote distance education through digital technologies while "maintaining an appropriate balance between the rights of copyright owners and the needs of users"

- States explicitly that nothing in this section shall affect rights, remedies, limitations, or defenses to copyright infringement, including fair use...".

(Library of Congress, 2007, www.loc.gov)

World Intellectual Property Organization Copyright Treaty (WCT)

The "WCT" obligates member states/nations of the World Trade Organization to prevent circumvention of technological measures used to protect copyrighted works, and to prevent tampering with the integrity of copyright management information. In part it states:

> "The contracting parties shall provide adequate and effective legal remedies against any person who knowingly performs any of the following acts............ "i) to remove or alter any electronic rights management information without authority; ii) to distribute, import for distribution, broadcast or communicate to the public, without authority, works or copies of works knowing that electronic rights management information has been removed or altered without authority".

It is a matter of best practice to have contractors assert, in their proposal, the restrictions that apply to the required end product. For example:

Computer Software To be furnished with Restrictions	Basis for assertion	Asserted Rights Category	Name of Persons/Entities Asserting Restrictions* (may be a third party)
LIST	LIST	LIST	LIST

The Federal Acquisition Regulations (FAR) require the following contract provision to delineate restrictions that may apply:

**Representation of Limited Rights Data and
Restricted Computer Software (May 1999)**

(a) This solicitation sets forth the work to be performed if a contract award results, and the Government's known delivery requirements for data (as defined in FAR 27.401). Any resulting contract may also provide the Government the option to order additional data under the Additional Data Requirements clause at 52.227-16 of the FAR, if included in the contract. Any data delivered under the resulting contract will be subject to the Rights in Data—General clause at 52.227-14 that is to be included in this contract. Under the latter clause, a Contractor may withhold from delivery data that qualify as limited rights data or restricted computer software, and deliver form, fit, and function data in lieu thereof. The latter clause also may be used with its Alternates II and/ or III to obtain delivery of limited rights data or restricted computer software, marked with limited rights or restricted rights notices, as appropriate. In addition, use of Alternate V with this latter clause provides the Government the right to inspect such data at the Contractor's facility.

(b) As an aid in determining the Government's need to include Alternate II or Alternate III in the clause at 52.227-14, Rights in Data—General, the offeror shall complete paragraph (c) of this provision to either state that none of the data qualify as limited rights data or restricted computer software, or identify, to the extent feasible, which of the data qualifies as limited rights data or restricted computer software. Any identification of limited rights data or restricted computer software in the offeror's response is not determinative of the status of such data should a contract be awarded to the offeror.

(c) The offeror has reviewed the requirements for the delivery of data or software and states [*offeror check appropriate block*]—

❏ None of the data proposed for fulfilling such requirements qualifies as limited rights data or restricted computer software.

❏ Data proposed for fulfilling such requirements qualify as limited rights data or restricted computer software and are identified as follows: _____

Protection Issues

Methods of Protection

Because software programs today are largely developed independent of the hardware, software developers have legal means by which rights related to software are protected. Contract administrators must ensure that end users are aware of the limitations associated with the use of software. There are four ways to protect intellectual property - patents, trademarks, copyrights or trade secrets. All are collectively referred to as intellectual property.

PATENT

A patent for an invention is the grant of a property right to the inventor, issued by the Patent and Trademark Office. The term of a new patent is 20 years from the date on which the application for the patent was filed in the United States or, in special cases, from the date an earlier related application was filed, subject to the payment of maintenance fees. US patent grants are effective only within the US, US territories, and US possessions.

The right conferred by the patent grant is, in the language of the statute and of the grant itself, "the right to exclude others from making, using, offering for sale, or selling" the invention in the United States or "importing" the invention into the United States. What is granted is not the right to make, use, offer for sale, sell or import, but the right to exclude others from making, using, offering for sale, selling or importing the invention (U.S. Patent and Trademark Office, 2007, www.uspto.gov).

TRADEMARK

A trademark is a word, name, symbol or device which is used in trade with goods to indicate the source of the goods and to distinguish them from the goods of others. A servicemark is the same as a trademark except that it identifies and distinguishes the source of a service rather than a product. The terms "trademark" and "mark" are commonly used to refer to both trademarks and servicemarks.

What is granted is...

the right to exclude

others from making,

using, offering for sale,

selling or importing

the invention.

Trademark rights may be used to prevent others from using a confusingly similar mark, but not to prevent others from making the same goods or from selling the same goods or services under a clearly different mark. Trademarks which are used in interstate or foreign commerce may be registered with the Patent and Trademark Office (U.S. Patent and Trademark Office, 2007, www.uspto.gov).

COPYRIGHT

Copyright is a form of protection provided to the authors of "original works of authorship" including literary, dramatic, musical, artistic, and certain other intellectual works, both published and unpublished. The 1976 Copyright Act generally gives the owner of the copyright the exclusive right to reproduce the copyrighted work, to prepare derivative works, to distribute copies or photo records of the copyrighted work, to perform the copyrighted work publicly, or to display the copyrighted work publicly.

The copyright protects the form of expression rather than the subject matter of the writing. For example, a description of a machine could be copyrighted, but this would only prevent others from copying the description; it would not prevent others from writing a description of their own or from making and using the machine. Copyrights are registered by the Copyright Office of the Library of Congress (U.S. Patent and Trademark Office, 2007, www.uspto.gov).

TRADE SECRETS

Trade Secrets are information that companies keep secret to give them an advantage over their competitors. The formula for Coca-Cola is the most famous trade secret (U.S. Patent and Trademark Office, 2007, www.uspto.gov).

Remedies

During contract administration, one of the most serious risks to the buyer is that the specified rights of the software supplier/developer are compromised through some action or inaction of the buyer/user organization. The rights afforded the developer by law and by contract vary. Recognize that each contract stands on its own; additional rights are briefly discussed.

A patentee may seek injunctive or administrative relief if they suspect or know that a buyer is making, using or selling outside the boundaries afforded by the contract. First and foremost, the patentee may seek injunctive relief which prohibits the buyer from continuing to engage in the cited activity. Additionally, patentees have rights under the Royalty Adjustment Act of 1942 which permits administrative settlements of royalty disputes. Administrative claims are generally less expensive to file as opposed to injunctive or judicial relief; however administrative filings do not provide the power of injunctive relief.

Traditional relief (administrative, judicial) may take the form of reasonable compensation based upon the number of infringements. That rate of compensation can be calculated from reasonable royalties that would have been due, lost profits, and savings that the state agency realized. Another remedy, "willing-buyer willing seller", calculates settlement upon the "knowledgeable, prudent business man" theory (i.e. a negotiation between the parties).

The diligence of the contract administrator in ensuring that end users are aware of the limitations of the rights of use will go a long way toward preventing software providers from seeking injunctive, judicial or administrative relief.

For the Buyer

Typically, buyers are concerned with the performance of the software, i.e intended use and form, fit and function. Contract warranties provide the ? in the event that the software fails to meet the conditions called for in the

Express Warranties

An express warranty can be a seller or manufacturer's oral or written promise or affirmation of fact which describes the product at the time of sale. This is a typical UCC express warranty; the seller's or manufacturer's written promise to repair or replace defective parts for a stated period of time; the seller's written promise containing representations that the product is defect free and/or a promise to repair or replace it.

Implied Warranties

The existence of an express warranty may void the argument that an implied warranty exists. Implied warranty of merchantability states that the product is suitable for its intended use.

(See Chapter 7 for a detailed discussion of Inspection, Acceptance and Warranties.)

Note that commercial software warranties are express in their limitations. Software is warranted to be free from defects that impair the promised operation of the software. One of the most difficult challenges during contract administration is to ascertain whether a defect exists. Common software defects are latent defects that are not discovered until the software has been accepted. Additionally, interoperability and interface issues among software programs and operating systems may impact the suitability of use for a specific software program.

To invoke rights under warranty provisions of the contract, the contract administrator must understand the rights granted under the licensing agreement and should, in most cases, be prepared to provide the steps which were followed when the failure occurred. This will allow the provider to repeat the procedure and determine if a defect actually exists.

"Oh, if only it were so simple."

Management and Enforcement of Service Level Agreements

Service level Agreements (SLAs) are performance-based instruments for acquiring and managing software contracts. SLAs can be used to specify software quality but are also often used to specify performance requirements. SLAs help to ensure that quality requirements are identified and established in the acquisition planning phase. SLAs assist contract administrators in establishing quality controls to monitor and manage the various aspects of software contracts. SLAs should carry sufficient weight so that buyers and suppliers focus their efforts on the aspects of the software that will enable the user organization to meet its organizational goals.

The ability of the contract administrator to effectively manage the software contract toward an outcome-focused goal is largely dependent on the requirements which were stated in the bidding documents. Those requirements must have a performance focus linked to:

- network performance
- disaster recovery
- problem management

- security
- storage solutions
- user management

The focus during contract administration should be on the quality of software performa~ in terms of resource utilization, security of software systems, reliability, and maintain~

Contract administrators must have a team in place to monitor planned performance outcomes such as monitoring the network, monitoring operating systems, identifying and assisting in problem resolution and warranty claim management.

SLAs can also be utilized for maintenance events when new versions of software are released or patches must be deployed. Contract oversight is made easier through the use of SLAs because they define the level of performance expected, how the performance will be measured, responsibilities of the parties and means to settle disagreements (Kendrick, 2003).

Sample Measurement Criteria of a SLA:

Reliability	Accuracy	Response Time	Problem Resolution
e.g. 95-98%	e.g. User error only	X time	X time

Contract Administration: Considerations for Software Contract Management:

1. Agreement and understanding of planned or anticipated software/hardware interfaces.
2. Use of formal inspections to ensure that defects that should be identified early in the process are identified.
3. Tracking of defects so that contract/license rights may be invoked.
4. Plan for correction of defects during performance.
5. Predefined metrics (measures of effectiveness) in terms of service levels.
6. Education of end users on contract rights and remedies.
7. Total contract visibility to ensure compliance with the contract.
8. Understand license agreements.
9. Have a software code of ethics.
10. Have all employees sign Employee Compliance Statements.
11. Establish a software register.
12. Keep original discs safely stored and locked.
13. Educate users.
14. Designate a software auditor.
15. Conduct unannounced software checks.

Additional Sources of Information

The Software Engineering Institute, Carnegie Mellon Institute (www.sei.cmu.edu/cmm/)

Best Manufacturing Practices Center of Excellence (www.bmpcoe.org)

Software Projects Institute (www.softwareprojects.org)

Applied Software Project Management by Andrew Stellman & Jennifer Greene (available at amazon.com)

Data Deliverables during a Contract

The topic of technical data stimulates discussion among practitioners and scholars of public procurement. Primary concerns focus on rights regarding technical data delivered under contracts. The longstanding policy within many public sector organizations has been exclusive rights to the public agency for all technical data delivered under a contract. However, such views have recently changed, as many public sector organizations attempt to reduce the barriers that commercial organizations associate with public procurement. Data can be expensive, and rights to technical data delivered under contracts are often the subjects of intense negotiations.

Any discussion of intellectual property would be exhaustive and is the subject of separate coursework. Accordingly, this section will provide a brief orientation on the following issues:

- The definition and parameters of technical data
- The rights to technical data
- Progress reports and cost data reports.

Technical Data

Definition and Parameters

Technical data is unique. It is data that relates to the technical performance, operability, manufacturing, maintenance, and support of systems. It also is associated with service contracts, because software programs that might be a by-product of a service contract are considered technical data. Technical data has significant potential value and is a critical component of the contract strategy and formulation process. Within the context of data, contract administration must ensure that any public agency rights to technical data are protected and enforced during contract performance and that the quality and timeliness of the data is consistent with contractual requirements.

Rights to Technical Data

There are three basic types of technical data rights which are commonly recognized.

Unlimited Rights. The public agency gains the right to use, reproduce, alter, and disclose the technical data as it sees fit. As previously stated, unlimited rights policies have proven to be a deterrent to other qualified suppliers bidding on public sector work. Technical data may contain trade secrets, which savvy suppliers are not inclined to release.

Limited Rights. The public agency retains the right to use the technical data under certain circumstances, as negotiated by the contracting parties. Typically, limited rights would provide the public agency with the right to share technical data within the agency (as bound by the contract terms and conditions), and the supplier would retain exclusive rights within the commercial marketplace. A restrictive legend would outline the limitations on the use of the data. Limited rights to technical data require thoughtful analysis of the conditions under which the public agency might find such data useful. Administrative problems can arise as the Contracting Officer seeks to protect the unauthorized disclosure or use of the technical data.

No Rights. The public agency retains no rights to technical data. This type of right is commonly found in contracts for commercial supplies and services. There may be limited exceptions that allow a public agency to retain rights to maintenance manuals and similar reference documents.

Other Data Deliverables

Outside the boundaries of technical data, other deliverables are commonly required under specific contract terms and conditions. Reports, such as progress and other administrative reports, are not considered technical data but are critical to the contract administration process.

Progress Reports

Progress reports may be included as a contract deliverable. During the contract phase, the Contract Administration Team is responsible for ensuring that such reports are delivered on time, in the format agreed to in the contract, and of a quality level consistent with industry standards.

Progress reports are a useful means of assessing the routine progress of the contractor in stated areas. They address those technical items that relate to the performance of the contract. Progress reports submitted by contractors can also be used to examine the quality assurance of the contractor. For example, the progress report can include metrics, which provide the Contracting Officer and the Contract Administration Team with useful data for assessing compliance with performance standards. They also serve as a "watch list" of sorts, because the progress reports "tell a story" of progress through the contract performance.

Progress reports can be required at any intervals stated in the contract. Common intervals for progress reports are bi-weekly, monthly and quarterly. The reports should be treated as "chapters in a book," because they tell the story of contract performance at stated intervals. Careful attention should be paid to the information contained in the progress reports to ensure that all significant actions that occurred during the reporting periods are discussed. Also, the reports should provide continuous discussion of action items that transcend reporting periods. For example, a pending action in February should be addressed in subsequent reports until it is resolved.

Cost Data Reports

The contract may contain special requirements for deliverables that address cost issues related to the contract. The amount of cost information provided in such reports will vary from contract to contract. For research and development efforts, extensive cost data may be a requirement, since no tangible product would likely result. However, contracts for the furnishing of commercial supplies would probably not contain any requirements for cost data. Cost data can be expensive, because contracts generally require cost accounting systems that accumulate and segregate data consistently.

The Contracting Officer must be aware of the data requirements stated in the contract so that compliance with the stated requirements can be effectively managed.

Appendix C is an excerpt from NASA's *Handbook on Contract Data* which provides an example of the considerations that must occur when determining data requirements.

References

Kendrick, T. (2003). Identifying and managing project risk: Essential tools for failure-proofing your project. New York: AMACOM.

Mann, C. (2002, July/August). *Why software is so bad.* Technology Review, 33-38.

Paulk, J. C., Curtis, B., Chrissis, M. B., & Weber, C. V. (2005). *The capability maturity model for software.* In R. H. Thayer & M. Dorfman (Eds.), Software engineering: The supporting processes (Vol. 2, 3rd ed.). Hoboken, NJ: John Wiley & Sons.

Rawicz, L., & Nash, R. C., Jr. (2001). *Intellectual property of government contracts* (5th ed.). Washington, DC: The George Washington University, Law School, Government Contracts Program.

Chapter 10

Delays in Contract Performance

Introduction

Unanticipated delays are one of the most common contract administration problems. Delays can adversely affect the goals and value of the public procurement function and result in:

- Failure of the entire project
- Redirection and disruption of both parties' efforts
- Decreased efficiency
- Increased cost.

Any combination of these end results will cost considerable tax dollars and erode the value of the public procurement profession. Accordingly, it is vital to minimize delays through effective, proactive measures within the supply chain so that the delivery of goods and services to the public sector and its constituency are consistent with contractual expectations. Equally important, the Contracting Officer needs to know their rights and limitations regarding compensatory claims resulting from delays. Essentially, a delay occurs when:

- The delivery period has passed and work has not been completed.
- The Contractor provides notification of an anticipated delay in delivery or performance that will result in failure to meet time performance requirements.

Failure by the contractor to meet a delivery schedule usually originates with problems that occurred earlier in the course of work. Therefore, progressive action should be taken as soon as a potential delay is identified so that responsibility and consequential costs can be allocated to one or both parties.

- Identify the existence of an actual or anticipated delay.
- Determine if the delay will impact delivery or performance.

- Determine fault.
- Determine duration of delay.
- Select appropriate action to resolve the problem.

Within the context of contractual delays, this chapter will explore the legal framework of three categories of delays: excusable, non-excusable, and compensable.

Excusable Delays

Definitions and Parameters

The excusable delay contract clause provides the contractor with protection from sanctions for late performance, such as default termination, liquidated damages, actual damages, and excess costs due to delays. If an excusable delay is granted, the contractor is generally responsible for bearing any increase in costs to perform the contract with the completion date extended to allow for the delay. The public agency is responsible for costs and time delays that it causes, has under its control, or for which it has agreed to pay the contractor, such as accelerated delivery if an excusable delay is granted.

Requirements for Consideration

In order for a delay listed in the default clause to be considered excusable, it must meet two general requirements.

The delay must be beyond the control of the Contractor. The first determination for an excusable delay is to determine if the cause of delay is beyond the control of the contractor. Three factors must be considered.

- *Was the delay unforeseeable?* The contractor is expected to be familiar with the industry for which the contract has been awarded. "Foreseeability" means the contractor should have adequate knowledge or reason to know the potential risks and has taken necessary steps to protect itself prior to submitting a bid. The mere fact that some unknown or unexpected event may occur does not constitute foreseeability. The contractor has the burden of proving that the delay could not have been foreseen.

- *Could the delay have been prevented?* If the contractor can prevent the event, the event can, therefore, be controlled. For example, if the contractor pulls resources from the job and allocates the resources to another high priority job, or if a contractor has a dispute with a subcontractor that causes work stoppage, these types of events are not beyond the contractor's control.

- *Can the consequences of the delay be overcome?* For supply contracts, a delay is not excusable if the contractor can obtain supplies from another source. The contractor must demonstrate that it is commercially and/or financially difficult to overcome the delay. Proving economic hardship by itself is not sufficient proof. If there is another source available, the contractor must provide the supplies, regardless of cost, unless the contractor can prove the cost is exorbitant.

The delay must be without the contractor's fault or negligence. The second determination for an excusable delay is to determine if the cause of delay was not due to the contractor's fault or negligence. Fault or negligence occurs when an act or omission by the contractor causes the delay, e.g., faulty wiring installed by the contractor starts a fire and causes damage which delays further progress.

Causes for Excusable Delays

A supply and/or service contract will likely recognize the following types of excusable delays:

Acts of God or of a Public Enemy (Force Majeure). Acts of God, as defined by the U.S Comptroller General, are a "singular, unexpected and irregular visitation of a force of nature." An example would be an earthquake. The death of the contractor's key employee is not an act of God.

Act of Public Agency in Either its Sovereign or Contractual Capacity. A sovereign act is defined as an action taken by the public agency for the common benefit and to enable or ensure the health, safety, or welfare of its citizens, e.g., the public agency grounds all air traffic for a period of time to protect national security. Conversely failure by the public agency to perform its contractual duties, cooperate, or not interfere are grounds for an excusable delay. For example, if the contract calls for inspection of a subsystem to be completed by a specific date and the public agency fails to do so, the contractor may have grounds for an excusable delay.

Fires, Floods, Epidemics, Quarantine Restrictions and Freight Embargos. In order to be considered as an excusable delay, a fire, flood, epidemic, quarantine restriction, and freight embargo must not be caused by contractor negligence.

Unusually Severe Weather. In order to be an excusable delay, the following condition must be met: The weather must be unusually severe causing critical work to be delayed. To qualify as unusually severe, the weather must be abnormal for that location for the same time period when compared to past weather conditions. Typically, government weather statistics for the location are used to make the determination. Harsh conditions, unless proven abnormal, are considered foreseeable. The contractor must also prove that the unusually severe weather actually impacted critical work.

Subcontractor Delays. For supply contracts, the contractor must demonstrate that the delay by the subcontractor was beyond the contractor's control and not the fault of any of the contractors. If the failure to perform is caused by the default of a subcontractor at any level, and if the cause of the default is beyond the control of both the contractor and subcontractor and without the fault or negligence of either, the contractor shall not be liable for any excess costs for failure to perform, unless the subcontracted supplies or services were obtainable from other sources in sufficient supply time for the contractor to meet the required delivery schedule.

Time Extensions and other Options for Excusable Delays

The contractor has the responsibility to prove that a delay is caused by an excusable event. Once a delay has been proven to be excusable, the length of the time extension must be established. A contractor is only entitled to time extensions directly related to the actual delayed performance that has been excused. For example, if the project or delivery is delayed by three days due to an act of God, the time extension for the new delivery or completion date should be only three days.

Depending on the impact and criticality of the requirement, the public agency may pursue one or more of the following options and accept responsibility for any increased costs.

- Accelerate delivery
- Allow substitution
- Change inspection location
- Allow other specification changes

Non-Excusable Delays

The following delays are generally considered non-excusable, because the contractor assumes the risk of providing the necessary amount of planning and effort to complete the contract:

- Financial difficulties
- Lack of materials
- Labor problems, excluding strikes
- Lack of equipment and facilities
- Lack of knowledge
- Foreseeable delays preceding award

Compensable Delays

A contractor may be able to receive compensation for increased costs as a result of a delay after consideration and documentation of the following factors:

- The cause of the delay
- The impact of the delay upon the contractor
- The compensable contract provision.

The Cause of Delay

In order for a contractor to receive compensation based on the cause of delay, one of the following conditions must exist:

Compensable Delay Clause. If the contract contains a compensable delay clause, it should clearly define the exclusive conditions for granting compensation to the contractor. If the contract does not contain a compensable delay clause, the contractor must demonstrate that the public agency caused the delay by interference, lack of cooperation or unreasonable breach of its contractual responsibilities.

Ordered Suspensions. If the public agency orders that work be suspended due to a provision in the Suspension of Work clause, the contractor may be compensated only if the resultant delay is unreasonable. For example, if the public agency suspends work due to faulty performance but fails to lift the suspension after accepting a correction, the contractor may be compensated. Contractors are not entitled to compensation if the suspension of work is the contractor's fault. For example, if the contractor did not furnish the required drawings for approval, resulting in project delays, the contractor is not entitled to compensation.

Constructive Suspensions. Constructive suspensions occur when the public agency is found to be responsible for the work stoppage and did not issue a suspension of work. The following are examples:

- *Public Agency Convenience*. If the delay is due to public agency convenience, such as correction of problems caused by a previous contractor, or if the agency has to determine how to deal with unforeseen conditions, the contractor cannot be expected to bear the risks and costs of the delay.

- *Delay in Issuing the Notice to Proceed*. If the public agency delays issuing a Notice to Proceed and a time or condition for issuance has been established, the public agency may be found to unreasonably delay the work.

- *Delays in Site Availability*. The contractor must demonstrate that there was an express warranty from the public agency because the site was supposed to be available at a specific time. If a condition of issuance of a Notice to Proceed is based on the availability of the site, the public agency has expressed a warranty of site availability.

- *Delay in Approvals*. The contractor must demonstrate that there is public agency fault or that an express warranty existed, such as delaying approval of ongoing work, if a time had been specified.

- *Funding Delays*. Non-appropriation of funds is not a compensable delay, but failure to provide the contractor with prompt information on the status of funding may be cause for a compensable delay.

- *Delays in Inspection*. Failure to conduct inspections at specified times and unreasonably delaying inspections are compensable delays.

- *Delays in Issuing Change Orders.* If there is a disagreement over the need for change requested by a contractor, the public agency has a reasonable amount of time to make a decision but will be liable for unreasonable delays.

References

Buffington, K. W., CPPO, C.P.M., & Flynn, M., Esq. (2007). *The legal aspects of public purchasing. (2nd ed.).* Herndon, VA: NIGP.

Case Study: Armed Services Board of Contract Appeals. From www.law.gwu.edu/ASBCA.

Cibinic, J. Jr., & Nash, R. C., Jr. (1995). *Administration of government contracts* (3rd ed.). Washington, DC: The George Washington University.

Federal Acquisition Regulations Web Site, www.arnet.gov/far/loadmainre.html.

Chapter 11

Disputes and Appeals

No matter how carefully a contract is negotiated and written, the complexities of the contracting process may cause disputes to occur. Many contracts contain some variation of disputes and claims clauses that provide the framework for how disputes will be resolved. The contracting parties agree, by the language in the written contract, how they will resolve disputes and claims that arise at some later date.

This chapter will explore the fundamental concepts and applications centering on contractual disputes and appeals by:

- Presenting reference clauses for disputes
- Presenting parameters, concepts and examples of disputes
- Contrasting disputes and claims
- Highlighting parameters for appeals
- Explaining the techniques, advantages, and disadvantages of Alternative Dispute Resolution (ADR)
- Offering guiding principles for conflict resolution.

Disputes

Disputes clauses are designed to facilitate the process in the event a disagreement cannot be resolved. The language of any disputes clause, in addition to providing the process framework for action, serves to encourage the parties to resolve disputes through the negotiation process to the maximum extent practicable.

Disputes clauses should include applicable procedures as well as the rights and responsibilities of both parties and should provide a procedure for appeal of the Contracting Officer's decisions. It should be identical to a disputes clause mentioned in the Request for Proposal document. The goal is to bring the contractor back into compliance with the contract.

It should be noted that public agency disputes clauses normally encompass disputes arising "under the contract" and those "relating to the contract." The effect of the latter component is to expand the scope of the dispute process to many claims for which no specific remedy is provided under a contract clause. As a result, the volume of litigation is potentially reduced. Other key provisions that should be considered for inclusion in disputes clauses include the following:

- The requirement that contractor claims must be submitted in writing to the Contracting Officer
- A time limit for issuance of a decision by the Contracting Officer
- The stipulation that decisions rendered by the Contracting Officer are final unless an appeal or suit is filed
- A time limit for filing an appeal
- A requirement that the contractor continue to perform pending final resolution of any request for relief, claim, appeal, or action arising under the contract, and comply with any decision of the Contracting Officer. Consideration should be given to expanding the stipulation to include claims related to the contract.

It should be noted that the definition of a dispute should be clear so that there is no confusion about whether or not a dispute exists. For example, mere failure to pay an invoice should not constitute a dispute; rather, disputes arise due to failed attempts to reach agreement on matters of disagreement.

References

The framework for resolving disputes that exists within the U.S. Federal Government contracting process is a good reference for public procurement agencies as they consider developing disputes clauses. The following clause was introduced in December 1998 for use in federal level contracts:

(a) This contract is subject to the Contract Disputes Act of 1978, as amended (41 U.S.C. 601-613).
(b) Except as provided in the Act, all disputes arising under or relating to this contract shall be resolved under this clause.
(c) "Claim," as used in this clause, means a written demand or written assertion by one of the contracting parties seeking, as a matter of right, the payment of money in a sum certain, the adjustment or interpretation of contract terms, or other relief arising under or relating to this contract. A claim arising under a contract, unlike a claim relating to that contract, is a claim that can be resolved under a contract clause that provides for the relief sought by the claimant.

However, a written demand or written assertion by the Contractor seeking the payment of money exceeding $100,000 is not a claim under the Act until certified as required by paragraph (d)(2) of this clause. A voucher, invoice, or other routine request for payment that is not in dispute when submitted is not a claim under the Act. The submission may be converted to a claim under the Act, by complying with the submission and certification requirements of this clause, if it is disputed either as to liability or amount or is not acted upon in a reasonable time.

(d) (1) A claim by the Contractor shall be made in writing and, unless otherwise stated in this contract, submitted within 6 years after accrual of the claim to the Contracting Officer for a written decision. A claim by the Government against the Contractor shall be subject to a written decision by the Contracting Officer.

(2) (i) The Contractor shall provide the certification specified in paragraph (d) (2)(iii) of this clause when submitting any claim exceeding $100,000.

(ii) The certification requirement does not apply to issues in controversy that have not been submitted as all or part of a claim.

(iii) The certification shall state as follows: "I certify that the claim is made in good faith; that the supporting data are accurate and complete to the best of my knowledge and belief; that the amount requested accurately reflects the contract adjustment for which the Contractor believes the Government is liable; and that I am duly authorized to certify the claim on behalf of the Contractor."

(3) The certification may be executed by any person duly authorized to bind the Contractor with respect to the claim.

(e) For Contractor claims of $100,000 or less, the Contracting Officer must, if requested in writing by the Contractor, render a decision within 60 days of the request.

This clause provides some specific guidance and ground rules as well as a clear delineation of the rights and responsibilities of the contracting parties. The crafting of any disputes clause should address the types of matters included within this clause.

The American Bar Association's Model Procurement Code, developed through involvement with and financial support from the National Institute of Governmental Purchasing (NIGP), provides a similar dispute mechanism. The Model Procurement Code allows a designated authority to resolve disagreements at a level below the Chief Procurement Officer or the head of the procurement agency. Administrative and judicial remedies afford the contractor the right of appeal in federal, state, and local municipalities (ABA, 2001).

Parameters, Concepts, and Examples of Disputes

Any disputes clause should be designed to mitigate disagreements between the public agency and the contractor and to ensure that contract performance is not disrupted while the matter in dispute is being resolved.

The designated Contracting Officer generally has the authority to resolve many contractual matters. If agreement can be reached between the two parties with regard to equitable adjustments resulting from rights in contract clauses, additional reimbursement for extra work performed, or monies due per negotiated terms and conditions, a bilateral agreement is negotiated. If the parties cannot reach agreement, resolution takes place under the procedures set forth in the disputes clause of the contract. Although different contracts may contain variations of disputes clauses, the general policies and procedures should have some commonality.

Any disputes clause should be designed to mitigate disagreements between the public agency and the contractor...

The Contracting Officer and members of the Contract Administration Team must understand how the disputes clause of a contract operates and under what circumstances it may be invoked. In effect, the disputes clause of the contract serves as a protective mechanism so that the contractor has a remedy available in the event that a dispute cannot be resolved with the designated Procurement Agent or Contracting Officer. It forces the public agency to address contract issues; and, in certain circumstances, the use of the disputes clause may result in a negotiated settlement.

Alternatively, the public agency, as a means of attempting to resolve a matter in disagreement, may also use the disputes clause of the contract. Consider the following example: The State of Virginia inadvertently pays the same invoice twice. It attempts to recoup the improper payment by informing the contractor of the overpayment and requesting that the funds be returned. Despite several attempts to recover the improper payment in an amicable way, the contractor fails to acknowledge the State's request. The State may elect to use the disputes clause of the contract as a means of seizing the funds, thus placing the contractor in the position of having to argue his right to retain the overpayment. Thus, the State, through the disputes clause, notifies the contractor of the matter in dispute and informs the contractor of its intent to recover the funds (perhaps by offsetting a future payment).

Contrasting Disputes and Claims

Discussion of the disputes clause requires that two concepts be understood: claim and dispute. Both of these terms have been the subject of litigation. (When is a claim a claim, and when is a disagreement a dispute?) A claim must meet the "test" of a claim as prescribed in the contract clause and any underlying statutory or regulatory definitions that may apply. As a general rule, a claim is for a specific sum of money. In contrast, a dispute is the term used to characterize a matter of disagreement that is not resolvable between the parties. In other words, the parties have attempted to resolve the matter in an amicable fashion, and one or both of the parties believe that a formal disputes process is the only path that remains.

A party sets the dispute process in motion by the written submission of a claim. This claim requires the other party to respond in a timely manner and render a decision. Routine requests for equitable adjustments, progress payments, etc., are not claims until it is established that the other party disputes the asserting party's right to recovery or the amount of recovery. For a dispute to exist, there must be some evidence supporting a disagreement or a controversy between parties.

The contract should describe the assertion of claims process. The claim must be sufficiently detailed to enable the other party to give reasonable consideration to the merits of the claim. The notice should give specific reasons for the assertion as well as what corrective action is requested and should be signed by the appropriate personnel. The claim should be acted on expeditiously because there is the danger that by not acting quickly enough, there could be implied acceptance of the work or claim.

For example, if there has been some event in the contract that constitutes a change, the result may be increased costs or a schedule extension (or both) for the contractor. The contractor may initially advise the public agency that it considers the direction as a change. It then submits a proposal for the changed work, commonly known as a Request for an Equitable Adjustment (REA). The contractor is generally obligated to perform the changed work as directed by the Procurement Agent or Contracting Officer while the REA is being reviewed and negotiated.

It is important for members of the Contract Administration Team to understand their role and responsibilities with respect to the receipt, handling, analysis, and negotiation of claims. Failure to conduct a timely evaluation and negotiation of an REA will result in difficult negotiations, because actual costs will likely be the subject of negotiation. However, the contractor has no incentive for cost control and efficiency, because it will most likely insist on reimbursement for all costs incurred.

In this example, the opportunity for a claim is evident. It could result from failure to conduct a timely negotiation (which places the contractor in a difficult cash control situation) or failure to recognize the contractor's view of the extent of costs to be reimbursed. The disputes clause of the contract serves as the mechanism with which the contractor can force a more timely resolution of the REA, and the public agency may be liable for payment of interest if the clause provisions permit accrual of interest on claims.

The public agency Contract Administration Team plays an important role in the claims process, because it is often necessary that technical analysis be thoroughly conducted in order to establish the validity of the claim. Once the members of the team have completed their evaluation and recommendation, negotiations may be considered appropriate. In such cases, these team members will play an important role during the negotiation process.

Failure to provide timely feedback on the contractor's claim can result in an appeal of the claim. Within the federal claims process, failure to acknowledge a claim over $100,000 (or provide a decision within 60 days) can be construed as a denial of the claim. The Model Procurement Code provides a 120-day window (or a longer period as may have been agreed to by the parties) in which the Procurement Agent or Contracting Officer must render a final decision. Failure to do so permits the contractor to act as if an adverse decision had been received.

In some circumstances, the evaluators of a claim may conclude that the basis of the claim is not valid. In such cases, the recommendation may be to deny the claim. The basis for such a recommendation must be well documented and based on rational judgment and analysis. If a claim is denied, the contractor must be notified in writing of the decision and the basis for the decision. The basis for the decision to deny the claim is important because it serves to provide sufficient information that will discourage the contractor from appealing the decision.

Appeals

As part of the formal claims process, a contractor can petition for review by a higher authority. The decision to "appeal" may be grounded in the contractor's belief that the final decision is flawed.

The disputes and appeals processes vary among the different types of public agencies. Regardless of the differences among the various procedures, the goal of the contracting parties should remain constant—fair and equitable treatment of the parties to the contract consistent with the terms and conditions of the contract.

As a means of examining the common framework used by most public agencies, the federal-level guidelines are worth examining. Within the federal contracting process, the contractor may appeal the final decision to the agency's Board of Contract Appeals within 90 days of receipt of the decision or, within 12 months of receipt of the decision, to the U.S. Court of Federal Claims. If the contractor fails to do so, the final decision stands. All parties involved must understand the appeal policies and procedures that govern the municipality so that claims are treated properly within the boundaries of the governing system.

Managing the Claims Process

Formal disputes can break down relationships and cause contractual problems. A good contract will provide some preliminary activities that seek to avoid a formal claim from ensuing.

In the event that any dispute arises between the parties, the designated Contracting Officer should provide the contractor with a written statement of its interpretation. This interpretation should be noted as final, if appropriate, or subject to negotiation. If it is provided as final and conclusive in all respects, the contract may provide the contractor with a right of a written appeal within designated days (e.g., five working days). The decision of the Contracting Officer on any such appeal should be made within a prescribed number of days (e.g., 5 working days) and should be characterized as final. Presumably, the contract obligates the contractor to continue contract performance while the dispute is being resolved. The contractor may then decide to accept the decision as a correct and binding interpretation of the contract or to file an appeal before the appropriate higher-level jurisdiction.

Throughout the process, including that time in which the contractor awaits the final decision by the Contracting Officer or the administrative or judicial resolution of the claim, the contractor, as bound by the contract terms and conditions, may be required to proceed diligently and in good faith with the performance of the contract as interpreted by the Contracting Officer in the "final decision."

Alternative Dispute Resolution (ADR)

Many contracts contain language regarding the use of an ADR as a means of resolving disputes and matters in conflict. There are various methods of resolving disputes in a non-judicial manner. While an ADR may not be ideal for all contractual disputes, when used appropriately, it can facilitate resolution of the dispute and preserve the relationship between the contracting parties.

Techniques Available

ADRs offer a wide array of techniques to resolve conflicts. Some techniques involve a neutral third party acting as a facilitator. Other techniques rely on advice from the neutral third party, while some utilize the neutral third party as a decision maker. In reviewing a conflict for ADR potential, pay close attention to choosing the appropriate technique. Generally speaking, it is best to use the least intrusive technique possible. In other words, use a neutral third party as a facilitator or evaluator before using a neutral third party as a decision maker. The influence the neutral third party has over the resolution of the conflict, the less cont parties have over the process. Some of the more common ADR techniques are:

Using the Neutral Third Party as a Facilitator through:

- Partnering
- Ombudsman
- Mini-trial
- Structured Negotiations
- Mediation

Using the Neutral Third Party as an Advisor through:

- Neutral Evaluation
- Summary Jury Trial
- Fact Finding
- Non-binding Arbitration

Using the Neutral Third Party as a Decider through:

- Binding Arbitration

Many public procurement organizations have policies and procedures concerning the processing of contract disputes and appeals. The trend has been to use ADR procedures to the maximum extent allowable by law. The public agency's policy is to try to resolve by mutual agreement all contractual issues in controversy at the Contracting Officer's level. These procedures may include such actions as fact-finding, negotiation, facilitation, mini-trials, mediation, or arbitration. Common types of ADRs include the following:

- *Mediation.* Under mediation, a neutral third party helps to resolve a dispute. The mediator does not have the authority to impose a decision on either party. When and if a satisfactory resolution is not reached, the parties may still pursue a lawsuit.

- *Arbitration.* Under arbitration, the parties agree to abide by the decision of the arbitrator(s). The arbitrator is selected directly by the parties or is chosen in accordance with the terms of the contract. When the parties elect to use arbitration, they agree to be bound by the decision of the arbitrator.

- *Partnering.* Under partnering, the contracting parties meet after the contract award has been made, but before work has begun on a project, to identify expectations and set goals. These meetings usually take the form of one- or two-day workshops held in neutral retreat facilities. Partnering agreements are effective when both parties perceive benefits to the completion of the procurement.

Under U.S. Federal Government regulations, contractors are required to provide the certification when submitting any claim, if an ADR technique is elected to handle a dispute (FAR 33.207[c]). Many organizations have trained ADR specialists in various disciplines. The Better Business Bureau is also available to resolve disputes between contractors and their customers and provides training in ADR. Training is also available from other organizations.

Advantages and Disadvantages of ADR

There are advantages and disadvantages to the use of ADR. Regardless of the Contracting Officer's decision as to the appropriateness of its use during contract performance, the officer can adopt the strengths within ADR without the use of formal intervention of a third party. The following factors favor the use of ADR:

- The law of determinative legal issues is well settled.

- The dispute is primarily factual.

- The position of each side has merit, but its value is overstated.

- The cost of litigating the dispute would exceed the potential recovery.

- No further discovery is required—or limited expedited discovery will suffice—for each side to assess its strengths and weaknesses.

- Avoidance of an adverse precedent is appropriate.

- A speedy resolution is desirable.

- The case lends itself to settlement before a board or through a court decision.

- A strong presentation will give one side or the other a more realistic attitude about the case.

- Trial preparations could be costly and protracted.

- A neutral third party could help diffuse the emotion or hostility that may inhibit an appropriate settlement of the dispute.

- The evaluation by a neutral advisor could help break the stalemate.

- There is a continuous relationship among the parties.

- The parties have indicated that they want to settle.

The following factors should be considered as indicative of a dispute that is not a good candidate for ADR:

- The dispute is primarily over issues of law.

- A decision with precedential value is needed.

- A significant policy question is involved.

- A full public record of the proceeding is important.

- The outcome would significantly affect non-parties.

- The costs of using an ADR procedure would probably be greater (in time and money) than the costs of pursuing litigation.

- The case involves a willful or criminal violation of law.

- The advantage of delay runs heavily in favor of one side.

- The other side has no motivation to settle.

- More time must elapse before each side's position and settlement possibilities can all be evaluated.

- There is a need for continuing board or court supervision of one of the parties.

- The other side may not be forthright in its ADR presentation.

- The case is likely to be resolved efficiently without assistance (e.g., settle, motion).

- The case involves fraud.

Guiding Principles of Conflict Resolution

The Contract Administration Team may be required to assist in resolving conflicts that arise during contract performance. There are some universal rules for conflict resolution that all team members should remember. These principles are adapted from those utilized by the Alternative Resolution Dispute Team of the Office of Naval Research.

Think Before Reacting. The tendency in a conflict situation is to react immediately in order not to lose the opportunity to respond. In order to resolve conflict successfully, it is important to think before reacting—consider the options, weigh the possibilities, etc. The same reaction is not appropriate for every conflict.

Listen Actively. Listening is the most important part of communication. If one does not hear what the other parties are communicating, conflict cannot be resolved. Active listening means not only listening to what another person is saying with words but also to what is said by intonation and body language. The active listening process also involves letting the speaker know that they have been heard, e.g., "What I heard you say is . . ."

Assure a Fair Process. The process for resolving a conflict is often as critical as the conflict itself. It is important to assure that the resolution method chosen as well as the process for affecting that method is fair to all parties to the conflict. Even the perception of unfairness can destroy the resolution.

Attack the Problem. Conflict is very emotional. When emotions are high, it is much easier to begin attacking the person on the other side than it is to solve the problem. Conflicts are resolved when the problem rather than the person is attacked. What is the problem that lies behind the emotion? What are the causes instead of the symptoms?

Responsibility. Every conflict has many sides, and there is enough responsibility for Attempting to place blame only creates resentment and anger that heightens any existing conflict. In order to resolve a conflict, each party must accept its own share of the responsibility and eliminate the concept of blame.

Use Direct Communication. Individuals should say what they mean and mean what they say. Avoid hiding the ball by talking around a problem. The best way to accomplish this is to use "I-Messages." With "I-Messages," individuals express their own wants, needs, or concerns to the listener. "I-Messages" tell others what is wanted or felt in a clear and non-threatening way. A "you-message" blames or criticizes the listener. It suggests that the listener is at fault.

Look for Interests. Positions are usually easy to understand, because individuals are taught to verbalize what they want. However, to resolve conflict successfully, each party must uncover why they want something and what is really important about the issue in conflict. Remember to look for the true interests of the all parties involved in the conflict.

Focus on the Future. In order to understand the conflict, it is important to understand the dynamics of the relationship, including the history of the relationship. However, in order to resolve the conflict, each party must focus on the future. What needs to be done differently tomorrow?

Options for Mutual Gain. Look for ways to assure that each party will be better off tomorrow than they are today. One party's gain at the expense of another only prolongs conflict and prevents resolution.

Conclusion

Regardless of the methodology used to handle disputes that arise under the contract, the Contracting Officer must ensure that the members of the Contract Administration Team understand and are able to effectively apply the contractual language related to disputes. Every effort should be made to resolve disputes in a negotiated manner that is in the best interest of the parties. Contract interpretation issues should be made cautiously and must be consistent with the original intent. Remember that interpretation issues should be consistent with the intent of the contractual language during the pre-award stage.

A spirit of cooperation and partnership will help to anticipate problems and proactively seek solutions to those problems. In doing so, the contractual relationship can be preserved for the betterment of the program.

Reference

American Bar Association (2001). *The 2000 model procurement code for state and local governments.* Washington, DC: American Bar Association.

Chapter 12

Contract Payment

Introduction

A ll contracts contain payment clauses that must be enforced during contract performance. Generally, payment for supplies and services is requested upon successful completion (and sometimes prior acceptance) of some portion or all of the work required by the contract. Naturally, contractors are particularly interested in the payment mechanisms contained in the contract because payment terms affect cash flow and afford the contractor the profit motivation commonly found in contract prices.

In some situations, payment is a form of financing, as funds paid by the public agency may be made available to contractors during performance of the work. In these circumstances, payment provisions (known as partial or progress payments) may be withheld or interrupted if the public agency believes that the contractor has not lived up to its contractual obligations.

The Contracting Officer is responsible for enforcing payment rights and responsibilities during contract administration. To effectively do so requires an understanding of the payment processes to be used, the individuals involved in that process, and knowledge of the contractual terms related to payment.

Accordingly, this chapter will highlight the various payment methods utilized in the public sector and the corresponding benefits and risks of each by discussing:

- Completion payments[1]
- Progress payments
- Advance payments
- Prompt payment terms
- Partial payments
- Milestone payments
- Withholding payments
- Commercial financing

Financial Compensation Mechanisms

The various types of payment mechanisms contained in contracts provide different types of financial compensation methods. It is important to consider that the method of financial compensation is closely related to working capital and risk. Several common types of financing (or payment methods) are discussed herein. Each contract contains one or more of these compensation methods, depending on the complexity and variety of the supplies and services to be provided.

An example of commonly used contract language regarding completion payment is as follows:

> Unless otherwise specified in this contract, payment shall be made on partial deliveries accepted by the Public Agency if:
> (a) "The Public Agency shall pay the contractor, upon the submission of proper invoices or vouchers, the prices stipulated in this contract for supplies delivered and accepted or services rendered and accepted, less any deductions provided for in this contract.
> (b) The amount due on the deliveries warrants it; or the contractor requests it and the amount due on the deliveries is at least x dollars or y % of the total contract price."

Completion Payment

The most common type of payment found in contracts is payment upon successful completion of the work. It provides for full payment after work required by the contract has been completed or delivered by the contractor and subsequently inspected and accepted by the public agency.

If this is the only payment clause in a contract, the contractor is essentially financing all work during performance of the contract until delivery is made and the items are accepted. Such a payment mechanism places no risk on the public agency because it is not contractually obligated to make any payments until acceptance of the supplies or services is tendered. For example, if a software upgrade has been successfully installed one year after the contract was executed and the public agency has tested and accepted the upgrade, the contractor may submit an invoice for the year's work at the price(s) stated in the contract. This type of payment mechanism places the contractor in the position of financing the work for the year during which the work is being performed. Accordingly, risk is a consideration for the contractor.

It should be noted that this clause also makes reference to a proper invoice. Generally, invoicing clauses are closely related to the payment mechanisms in the contract. Therefore, care must be taken to examine and understand the invoicing instructions that the contractor is obligated to follow. A proper invoice may require, among other things, that a public agency representative certify the invoice, indicating that the supplies or services have been received and accepted. Such a certification may be a condition of invoice submission for payment. This form of checks and balances is common and ensures that payment is not made for items not accepted. It should be noted that this system of checks and balances can be most efficient within automated procurement and financial systems that link the ordering process with the receiving and payables process through electronic approvals.

Partial Payments

Partial payment methods permit the contractor to invoice the public agency at intervals that coincide with the delivery and acceptance of incremental supplies and/or services. In the previous example, partial payment provisions would permit the contractor to submit an invoice for software program updates as they were completed, delivered, and accepted by the public agency. Partial payments are commonly found in contracts that permit the incremental delivery of supplies. As supplies are delivered and accepted, payment can be requested only for those items that have been delivered and accepted. A contract for 1,000 workstations that requires delivery of 100 workstations each month would include partial payment provisions to permit the contractor to submit an invoice for payment upon the monthly delivery and acceptance of the 100 workstations.

...the method of financial compensation is closely related to working capital and risk.

Progress Payments

Progress payments permit the contractor to submit invoices for payment as progress is made in performing the contract. For example, as a software program is being updated and installed, the contractor might be permitted to request progress payments on a monthly basis as progress continues in the development of the software upgrade. Progress payment clauses will normally place limits on the total amount that can be invoiced and paid. A common value is 80% of the total price of the contract. The remaining 20% is typically set aside for payment at total contract completion.

Progress payments generally require that the contractor limit its invoice to those costs for which it has made payment. This means that expenses borne by the contractor for supplies, equipment, subcontractors, employees, and ancillary goods and services must be paid by the contractor before it can request payment from the public agency. The Contracting

Officer is cautioned to ensure that costs submitted for progress payment are examined for reasonableness, allow ability, and allocability to the contract.

Progress payment clauses require due diligence during contract administration to ensure that payments are consistent with the level of progress actually made in performance of the required work. Progress payments should be examined by looking at costs incurred and also at the level of progress achieved. Doing so ensures that the level of payment requested is commensurate with the progress actually made in performing the work.

Progress payment mechanisms shift the risk to the public agency because payment for progress made does not guarantee that work will be successfully completed. In fact, some contracts that experience performance problems view progress payment mechanisms as a means to over-fund (increase the price of the work) and "guarantee" success. Because of such dangers, the percentage of work determined to be complete in conjunction with the progress payment process should be compared to actual costs incurred by the contractor to ensure that the level of payment provided by the public agency is consistent with the level of effort provided by the contractor. In this way, the Contracting Officer can examine the relationship between the two financial benchmarks in terms of progress towards completion.

Milestone Payments

Milestone payments are a more sophisticated form of progress payment that shifts the risk by tying such payments to the successful completion of predetermined milestones that are deemed significant indicators of progress toward contract completion.

For example, operational testing of a software system may be identified as a milestone for which a representative of the public agency can authorize a payment. The challenge is to ensure that success at the stated milestone is validated. The milestones and the contractual value associated with each milestone should be contained in the contract, thus, eliminating the need to negotiate each milestone value during contract performance. Milestone payments place risk on both parties because the contractor can only request payment upon successful completion of the milestone. The public agency, on the other hand, continues to bear some risk because some contract value is associated with each milestone achieved. Payment is made to the contractor based on this achievement while final completion of the total contractual requirement is still pending.

Advance Payments

␣e payments pose the most risk for the public agency. As such, they are not the payment ␣hoice. Advance payments are made in advance of the start of contract performance ␣es or services not yet performed. Typical use of advance payment provisions occurs in situations where the contractor must make a significant capital investment for which it is unable to secure funds from other sources.

Under this scenario, the public agency would pay "in advance" of performance in order to fund a capital investment, thereby giving the contractor the capability of initiating contract work. For example, a contractor may require a CAD/CAM machine to perform the work required by the contract. The machine may represent a significant capital investment that cannot be funded by the contractor because he/she is a small business owner. The public agency would agree to advance the contractor the funds necessary to purchase the machine so that work could commence.

If advance payments are authorized under the contract, the Contracting Officer must ensure that the cost of the purchase is closely examined for reasonableness. Under most circumstances, the title to the equipment remains with the public agency unless other title and use provisions apply. Again, advance payments are the least preferred method of financing, because all the risk shifts to the public agency.

Other Payment Terms

Withholding of Payments

Many contracts contain various clauses that permit the public agency to withhold payment during contract performance for various reasons. Withholding of payment rights must be examined and understood by the Contract Administration Team. For example, a withholding-of-payment clause might permit the public agency to withhold 10% of the total payment due for the contractor's failure to provide data required by the contract. Under such a scheme, the contractor would not receive the remainder of the monies due under the contract until such time as the data has been tendered and accepted.

A withholding-of-payment clause must not be punitive and should bear some measure of reasonableness. Monies withheld pursuant to contract terms are not subject to interest under the Prompt Payment Act.

Prompt Payment Act

The Contracting Officer should verify whether the public agency is subject to prompt payment provisions. In 1982, the U.S. Federal Government enacted the Prompt Payment Act to ensure that the Federal Government paid their invoices in a timely manner. Cash flow and the expectation of payment in accordance with the terms of the contract is critical to a contractor's continued financial health. The Act requires that proper invoices (as defined in the contract) are to be paid within 30 days of receipt by the federal agency. It prescribes an interest "penalty" that accrues from each day beyond the 30-day period in which the invoice is not paid. Interest is computed at the U.S. Treasury rate in effect at the time. If the invoice is in dispute, payment will not be required in accordance with Prompt Payment Act provisions. In addition, some states have adopted Prompt Pay Policy acts to ensure timely payment with state-specific qualifying language and details.

Of particular interest is the statutory requirement for payment of interest without the contractor requesting or demanding the interest. The public agency is obligated, on its own, to compute and pay the interest due without any prodding from the contractor.

Contracting Officers must ensure that those personnel who participate in the invoicing process are aware of these statutory provisions and their responsibilities during the invoicing process. Prescribed duties regarding reviewing, approving, and processing proper invoices for payment should not place the public agency in the position of paying interest.

Commercial Financing

The preferred method of financing is commercial financing. Commercial financing places the contractor in the position of securing financing outside of the contractual relationship with the public agency. Under such terms, the public agency bears no risk associated with interim payment schemes. Because the contractor has secured commercial financing, payment by the public agency should occur after satisfactory performance and submission of a proper invoice by the contractor.

Assignment of Claims

Assignment of claims is the transfer by a contractor to a bank, trust company, or other financing institution, as security for a loan to the contractor, of its right to be paid by the government for contract performance. Small businesses may find that assignment of claims related to a specific contract improves or facilitates cash flow that ensures ongoing acceptable contract performance.

Assignment of claims for money due under a contract should only be honored if they have been received from a bank, trust company, or other financial institution.

Assignment documentation normally consists of two parts:
1. Notice of Assignment, which is completed by the financial institution.
2. Instrument of Assignment or Assignment of Claims, which is completed by the vendor/contractor.

Assignment documents should be notarized. Contract administrators should ensure that sufficient original, notarized copies are received to permit forwarding copies to internal payment organizations and other offices as required. One original copy should remain with the official contract file.

Contract administrators must ensure that if any assignments of claims have been made either as a condition of contract award (i.e. a qualification audit) or after the contract is signed, proper payment takes place in accordance with the assignment. Suggested steps are:

1. Review the contract (and proposal) and review and examine any notice of assignment, instrument of assignment, and assignment order(s) to determine that the assignment documentation has been properly executed.

2. Record the task order, purchase order, or delivery order number (AG#) and the original contractor vendor code on the assignment documentation.

3. Create a cover letter or transmittal form providing the name, address, and telephone number of a contact person (for problems related to the assignment and to whom an acknowledgement letter can be sent).

4. Submit notarized original assignment documents to payment office and other offices as required.

Liability for payments to the third party begins with acknowledgement of receipt of the assignment.

Part IV: Contract Administration Closure

Chapter 13

Contract Termination

Introduction

S uccessful contract administration requires that disputes be handled tactfully, effectively, and in a timely manner. There are many issues that can lead to claim submissions. A goal of contract administration is to settle claims by mutual agreement. Small claim issues quickly escalate into large claim issues if not handled promptly. Termination is a drastic adjustment of the contractual relationship and may be grounds for future litigation. Disputes, appeals, and termination actions test the mettle of the procurement and contract administration personnel.

The Contracting Officer will at some point in time deal with issues concerning the contractor's poor performance. The Procurement Department should, as a matter of course, proactively include clauses in the solicitation documents and contractual documents that protect the public agency from poor contractor performance by including warranties, performance bonds, liquidated damages, termination for convenience, and other legal remedies.

Termination procedures should begin only after thoughtful consideration of the consequences and with input from a variety of sources, such as legal counsel and the impacted governmental agencies. Discretion should be exercised when terminating for default to ensure that this is the best course of action, that no excusable condition exists, and that the right to terminate has not been waived through some unintentional action.

Although contract termination is an exhaustive topic of concern for Contracting Officers, this chapter will highlight the following key concepts:

- Termination for default due to a breach of contract
- The right to terminate for default

- Procedural notification requirements when terminating for default
- Appeals and waivers applied to a termination for default
- Consequences of a termination for default
- Alternatives to a default termination
- Termination for convenience: definitions and parameters
- Use of liquidated damages

Termination for Default due to Breach of Contract

D espite the best efforts, poor performance issues will still surface and must be dealt with proactively and aggressively. The key to handling poor performance problems is to manage relationships with contractors successfully.

Donald Harney (1992), in his textbook, *Service Contracting—A Local Government Guide*, has identified a progressive five-step plan for dealing with poor performance as it relates primarily to service contracts.

- **First step**: The field manager attempts to resolve the problem by working directly with the Contractor's on-site supervisor. In this way, the problem is being resolved directly at the site where the conflict occurs and amongst first line managers and supervisors. If the performance does not improve . . .

- **Second step**: The field or contract manager (or possibly the Contracting Officer, if warranted) contacts the Contractor to resolve the performance issues. If the performance does not improve . . .

- **Third step**: A more formal meeting with the project manager, the Contractor and Contracting Officer as well as the Procurement Agent is convened. The Procurement Department representative usually chairs the meeting and, if the performance problem is severe, legal representation might also be included. If the performance does not improve...

- **Fourth step**: ...[Action is initiated according to the contract provisions and applicable law, which could include liquidated damages or cure notice.]... If enforcement does not produce the desired result, the process moves to the fifth step.

- **Fifth step**: Contract termination is pursued. The goal in correcting poor performance is to bring about a change in behavior but when this fails the final resolution has to be contract termination. The nature of the problem and its impact on service delivery determine how and with what speed a performance problem is handled.

Despite the use of clear, progressive steps in contract monitoring that could lead to termination for default, it should be understood that contract termination is always problematic and very ·ky. If the contractor contests the termination, the public agency must have supporting documentation strong enough to sustain the termination. If the contract required a performance bond, the bonding company will demand pertinent documentation outlining the public agency's position. The agency should remember that the bonding company is an agent of the contractor and will not protect the interests of the public agency. In fact, it is not unusual for a bonding company to defend the actions of the contractor and refuse to satisfy the public agency's claim of contractor default. When the bonding company refuses to agree with the public agency's claim, negotiation with the bonding company or litigation may be the only recourse (Harney, 1992).

A discussion of what constitutes a breach of contract should be examined through a review of applicable laws and statutes. In the United States, contractual issues are addressed in the Uniform Commercial Code (UCC). This Code will be referenced throughout this chapter as illustrative examples of contract law. Nevertheless, similar federal or central government laws should exist in other nations. For example, the Canadian Government references the Uniform Sale of Goods Act, which is analogous to the UCC

Keep in mind that both the Uniform Commercial Code in the United States and the Uniform Sale of Goods Act in Canada govern domestic transactions between buyers and sellers. As public procurement seeks international markets for products and services, the Contracting Officer should become familiar with the United Nations Convention on the International Sale of Goods (CISG), which governs the sale of goods between nations.

Section 2-301 of the UCC provides that the basic obligation of the seller is to deliver conforming goods, and the basic obligation of the buyer is to accept and pay for conforming goods delivered by the seller. Therefore, by definition, a seller's breach of contract would be the failure to properly deliver conforming goods to a buyer, and a buyer's breach of contract would be the failure to accept and pay for conforming goods delivered by the seller. Regardless, both the seller and the buyer must provide notice to the other that a breach of contract has occurred.

The determination of whether a breach of contract by either party has occurred can be tricky. UCC Section 2-610 recognizes that a buyer or seller may, prior to when the performance of a contract obligation is due, refuse to perform a contract obligation. This refusal to "perform a contract obligation not yet due" amounts to an anticipatory repudiation of a contract. In this instance, either a buyer or seller may choose to apply Section 2-609 of the UCC by seeking, in writing, adequate assurance from a party that it will honor its contractual obligation. The failure on the part of either a buyer or seller to provide this assurance of performance within a reasonable time, not to exceed 30 days, will amount to repudiation of a contract.

Under UCC Section 2-611, a buyer or seller may retract a repudiation of a contract by providing a clear indication to the other party that the repudiating party intends to perform its contract obligations. Such retraction of a repudiation of a contract will be effective, unless the non-repudiating party has already canceled the contract or otherwise changed its position in reliance on the repudiation.

Sections 2-601 and 2-602 of the UCC provide further direction on notification and cure of a breach of contract in conjunction with the Buyer's Rightful Rejection of Goods. These provisions of Article 2 define the buyer's right to reject goods delivered by the seller if the goods fail to conform to the contract for any reason and also require the buyer to notify the seller of rejection of the non-conforming goods in a timely manner.

The *Seller's Right to Cure a Non-Conforming Delivery of Goods* is addressed in UCC Sections 2-508 and 2-608(3). The seller's right to cure is, perhaps, the best example of how far UCC Article 2 will go to give the buyer and seller a chance to complete a deal. The seller has two different Article 2 rights to "cure" (to correct a seller's delivery of non-conforming goods). If the time for performance by the seller under the contract has not expired and the seller has received notice of a rightful rejection or revocation of acceptance of the goods by the buyer, the seller, upon notice to the buyer, can make a delivery of conforming goods before the seller's time for performance expires. Where the buyer rejects or revokes acceptance of non-conforming goods delivered by the seller and the seller reasonably believed that the buyer would accept the non-conforming goods with or without some money adjustment, the seller, upon timely notice to the buyer, may have a reasonable time to deliver conforming goods to the buyer. In either case, if a seller notifies a buyer that it intends to cure the non-conforming delivery of goods and if the seller does, in fact, cure this non-conforming delivery, the buyer must accept the "cured delivery."

The Right to Terminate for Default

The right to terminate for default hinges upon two prerequisites: (1) reasonable grounds for termination or (2) noncompliance with certain procedural notification requirements.

Reasonable Grounds for Default Termination

There are two key issues to consider when determining whether the public agency has reasonable grounds to terminate a contract based on a default or breach of contract by the Contractor. Keep in mind that the public agency cannot issue a default termination arbitrarily.

Did the contractor fail to perform or deliver within the prescribed time period? The fundamental condition warranting a default termination is a failure of the contractor to perform the necessary work in accordance with the required contract specifications or a failure to deliver within the prescribed time period. The doctrine of "substantial compliance" prevents the public agency from terminating the contract due to poor performance without giving the contractor a reasonable period of time to cure the deficiencies. Further, to qualify for "substantial completion," the contractor must have completed the work within the prescribed time period, or had reason to believe that the goods or services conformed to the contract specifications, or had reason to believe that any defects were minor in nature and easily correctable. The basic test for determining if the defects are minor in nature is whether the product or service is capable of being used or occupied by the public agency for its intended purpose.

Did the contractor fail to make progress? As the second prerequisite for invoking the right to terminate a contract, the public agency may pursue default termination when the contractor's failure to make progress endangers the performance of the contract. This type of termination requires the public agency to prove that there is a reasonable likelihood that the contractor will not complete performance prior to the delivery date. The following factual considerations must be evaluated:

> *...the public agency cannot issue a default termination arbitrarily.*

- *Percentage of Completion and Time Remaining.* Each contract requires careful review before making this determination. The more complex the product or service, the greater the likelihood of default if a substantial amount of time has elapsed and only a small percentage of the contract has been performed. Direct comparison of the amount of work completed to the amount of time remaining is not always an accurate measure of when performance is endangered. The remaining work may be completed at a faster rate because the initial phase included necessary preparations or delays in the receipt of material required for final completion.

- *Consistent Quality Failure.* This means the consistent failure by the contractor to produce a product or service that meets the contract specifications.

- *Other Key Factors.* This could include the loss of key personnel and the failure to provide progress reports.

Procedural Notification Requirements

The procedural requirements that must precede a default termination are set forth in UCC Sections 2-309 and 2-610. These procedures focus on the obligation to give proper notice to the contractor of its deficiencies and the potential consequences. There are three types of notices usually listed in the termination clause.

Cure Notice

In a termination for default, if the contractor fails to perform some provisions other than those dealing with the timely delivery, or fails to make progress as to endanger performance altogether, the public agency must give the contractor written notice of the failure and allow a specified time for cure (remedy) of the failure before issuing a termination notice. The public agency should reserve the right, unilaterally, to extend the time for cure if it is in the best interest of the public agency without waiving the right to default. The cure notice should include all of the following, as appropriate:

- It should state that a termination for default may arise unless the failure to perform or make adequate progress is cured within a reasonable number of days. The notice must quantify the number of days.

- It should call the contractor's attention to its contractual liabilities in the event of default.

- It should request a written explanation of the failure to perform.

- It should state that failure to present an explanation may be interpreted as an admission that there is no valid explanation.

- It should invite the contractor to discuss the matter at a conference if appropriate.

- It should require the contractor to inform the public agency's designated representative of how it intends to cure the deficiency.

An example of instructions for issuing a Cure Notice by the U.S. Federal Government is contained in their Federal Acquisition Regulations (FAR 49.607[a]), which reads as follows:

> If a contract is to be terminated for default before the delivery date, a Cure Notice is required by the default clause. Before using this Notice, it must be ascertained that an amount of time equal to or greater than the period of the "cure" remains in the contract delivery schedule or extension to it. If the time remaining in the contract delivery schedule is not sufficient to permit a realistic "cure" period of 10 days or more, the Cure Notice should not be issued. The Cure Notice may be in the following format:

> Cure Notice
> You are notified that the Government considers your (specify the Contractor's failure or failures) a condition that is endangering performance of the contract. Therefore, unless this condition is cured within 10 days after receipt of this notice (or insert any longer time that the Contracting Officer may consider reasonably necessary), the Government may terminate for default under the terms and conditions of the (insert clause title) clause of this contract.

Show Cause Notice

The Contracting Officer may issue a Show Cause Notice prior to issuing a termination for default. The Show Cause Notice will notify the contractor of the reasons for the default and the consequences of a termination for default. The Notice will also request that the contractor "show cause" why the contract should not be terminated for default and will provide the contractor an opportunity to discuss the reasons for the problems. Failure of the contractor to provide an explanation may be taken as an admission that no explanation for the "cause" exists. An example of a Show Cause Notice is contained in FAR 49.607(b), which reads as follows:

> Since you have failed to (insert contract name) within the time required by its terms: or "cure" the conditions endangering performance under (contract name), the Government is considering terminating the contract under the provisions for default of this contract. Pending a final decision in this matter, it will be necessary to determine whether your failure to perform arose from causes beyond your control and without fault or negligence on your part. Accordingly you are given the opportunity to present, in writing, any facts bearing on the question to (Contracting Officer), within 10 days after receipt of this notice. Your failure to present any excuses within this time may be considered as an admission that none existed. Your attention is invited to the respective rights of the Contractor and the Government and the liabilities that may be invoked if a decision is made to terminate for default.

Notice of Termination for Default

Once the Contracting Officer determines termination for default is proper, the contractor will be issued an official written Notice of Termination containing the following information:

- The contract number, effective termination date, and description of the acts or omissions that constitute the default

- Contractor's appeal rights

- A statement that the contractor's right to proceed with performance of the contract (or a portion of the contract) is terminated

- If the Contracting Officer has not determined whether the failure to perform is excusable, the notice should state that it is possible that the contractor will be held liable for any excess costs the public agency must pay in re-purchasing terminated supplies or services

- If the Contracting Officer has determined that the failure to perform is inexcusable, the notice should state that (1) the notice of termination con⸍ such a determination and is a final decision under the termination for d⸍

clause; (2) the contractor will be held liable for any excess costs of re-purchase; and (3) delivered materials not incorporated are to become the property of the public agency.

Procedures for Proper Handling of Default Terminations

In addition to these notice procedures, the public agency should implement procedures to ensure timely and proper handling of default terminations. For example, notices should be sent via certified mail with return receipt requested. When a termination notice is issued, the fiscal officer should be advised to suspend additional payments pending further instructions. The contract file should always be documented to explain and justify the reasons for termination, and a copy of the termination notice should be sent to any surety of the contractor.

...a termination

for convenience

is a final action.

As an example, if a contractor receives Notice of Termination and the notice does not say whether it is a termination for default or convenience, the contractor believes it to be a termination for convenience and acts accordingly. The courts have issued decisions where, under these circumstances, it would be considered a termination for convenience. Accordingly, a termination for default should not be called a termination for convenience in order to protect the contractor's reputation. It should be understood that a termination for convenience is a final action. It cannot be changed to a termination for default at a later date. Finally, a terminated part of a contract may be reinstated, but only with the contractor's written permission.

Appeals and Waivers of Termination for Default

Contractor Rights to Appeal

The contractor has the right to appeal any decision. The appeal must be made within the time specified in the Termination for Default notice.

Waiver of Termination Rights

If the public agency encourages the contractor in some way to continue performance and, in reliance upon this inducement, the contractor does continue, a waiver may be found to have occurred. The following conditions may create a waiver by the public agency to the right to terminate for default:

- Approving a revised schedule, if the contractor follows the approved schedule
- Entering into negotiations for, or issuing a change order to, the contract, if a new delivery date is required but not established
- Indicating a willingness to have the contractor continue performance by stalling for an unreasonable length of time before beginning
- Termination actions or making express statements to the contractor about delinquency that leads the contractor to believe the late completion is forgiven.

Following a waiver, and in order to assert that time is important, the right to terminate must be re-established by issuing a written notice of the new completion date.

Consequences of Termination for Default

When exercising the right to terminate a contract for default, the public agency effectively informs the contractor that the performance failure has caused the public agency to terminate the agreement as set forth in the contract. A termination for default exposes the contractor to potential financial liability. There are several issues for the public agency to contemplate before terminating for default.

- For the contractor, the consequences of a default termination can be very serious—so the decision should not be taken lightly.
- Termination for default may not be in the public agency's best interest—there are alternatives.
- Termination for default cannot be done arbitrarily—such a decision must be preceded by certain conditions and procedures.

Intervening factors, such as improper notification or a waiver of termination rights, can render a default termination inappropriate or unenforceable.

Impact on Contractor

The impact of a default termination will vary, depending on a number of considerations. The most important of these is the type of contract. For example, the potential consequences to a contractor of a default termination under a fixed-price contract are far more serious than under a cost-reimbursement contract. While any default termination threatens the contractor's opportunity for future business, under cost-reimbursement contracts, the contractor can be assured of payment for all allowable costs regardless of whether or not the public agency accepts the work. The contractor is also entitled to a prorated percentage of the negotiated fee if the public agency accepts any portion of the work. However, under a fixed-price contract, a contractor faces the following consequences:

- *Financial Impacts.* The public agency is not liable for the costs of unaccepted work, and the contractor is only entitled to compensation for accepted work. Further, the public agency can demand the return of progress or partial payments. Additionally, the public agency has the right, but not the duty, to appropriate the contractor's material, inventory, and construction plant and equipment at the site, subject to negotiated compensation. Finally, the contractor is liable for excess costs of re-procurement or completion and may be liable for actual or liquidated damages.

- *The Loss of Future Public Sector Contracts through Debarment or Suspension.* If a contractor defaults on a contract, public procurement officials will normally enact debarment or suspension against a defaulting contractor.

  - **Debarment** is the exclusion of a person or company from participating in a procurement activity for an extended period of time, as specified by law, because of previous illegal or irresponsible action.
  - **Suspension** is the temporary exclusion of a person or company from participating in a procurement activity because of previous illegal or irresponsible action.

In many jurisdictions, debarment and suspension are very difficult to achieve because of political reasons. Recognition of this potential difficulty by the Contracting Officer reinforces the importance of recognizing the warning signs of poor performance and taking effective corrective action prior to the termination of a contract.

Impact on the Public Agency

Termination for default has the following impact on the public agency as well:

- Delays in obtaining necessary goods and services
- Potential difficulty in collecting excess re-procurement costs
- Expenditure of considerable time and effort defending a default termination.

Alternatives to a Default Termination

Although the public agency has the right to terminate, it does not mean that it should necessarily do so. Termination for default is rarely a satisfactory solution to unacceptable ce. Termination for default should be a decision of last resort. Unless another s able to provide the needed goods and services in a much shorter time than the ontractor, the public agency may choose to work with the existing contractor oblems. Terminating for default will not solve critical needs and, in certain instances, alternatives are not available. Terminating for default will do nothing to promote timely delivery of the agency's requirements. Therefore, before terminating for default, the public agency should consider the following:

- Whether it would be effective to withhold payment until satisfactory performance is demonstrated
- Whether, if termination action is taken, there is an alternative source of supply
- Whether the Contractor's financial condition precludes recovery for the excess cost of re-procurement
- Whether continued performance under a revised delivery schedule would better serve the public agency's interests
- Whether a no-cost termination agreement should be executed if the requirement for the supplies or services no longer exists and the contractor is not liable for damages.

Termination for default should be a decision of last resort.

Termination for Convenience

Parameters and Considerations

The Termination for Convenience clause allows the public agency to terminate a contract without cause and limits the contractor to recovering costs and profit on work completed and in preparation of the termination settlement. The contractor is not allowed to recover any anticipated profits that will not be realized as a result of termination. An example of a Termination for Convenience clause can be found in FAR 52.249-2[a]), which reads as follows: "The Government may terminate performance of work under this contract in whole or, from time to time, in part if the Contracting Officer determines that a termination is in the Government's interest."

Careful consideration should be given before including a Termination for Convenience clause. Depending on the type of product or service purchased, the contractor may not respond to a solicitation containing a termination for convenience clause, or may increase their offer accordingly. For example, a contract for a lease of equipment that includes a Termination for Convenience clause may include higher pricing due to contractual risks because the contractor has no assurances that the buyer will continue lease payments for the life of the contract.

Termination for convenience is most commonly exercised when the Contracting Officer determines that the product or work is no longer needed. The reality is that the contractor does not need to do anything wrong but can still be subjected to termination for convenience without any recourse. In accordance with provisions of any termination clause, the public agency must give written notice to include:

- the contract number
- a statement that the contract is being terminated for convenience
- effective termination date
- scope of the termination.

Termination Settlement

Following receipt of notice, the contractor must stop work immediately, terminate any subcontracts, and prepare a termination proposal. The public agency is obliged to negotiate an equitable termination settlement in an expeditious manner. The termination settlement negotiations focus on determining which of the following allowable cost items the contractor may be entitled to:

- commonly stocked items used in production of contract
- costs continuing after termination
- initial costs
- loss of value of assets;
- rental costs;
- subcontract claims
- termination inventory
- settlement expenses
- profit on partial work completed.

No-Cost Termination

When it is in both of the parties' best interests, the contract may be terminated for convenience without cost to either party.

Liquidated Damages

The termination options discussed thus far are intended to motivate the contractor to deliver what was promised by imposing severe financial consequences. A liquidated clause is intended to motivate the contractor to deliver on time by assessing less tary damages for each day of delay. The buyer's legal right to assess liquidated ated in UCC Section 2-718(1).

liquidated damages clauses are included in construction contracts but may be applicable to some supply and service contracts. In general, fixed liquidated damages clauses should be included in contracts when there is an expectation that damages will incur if performance is delinquent and when it is difficult or impossible to prove the amount of damage actually incurred. Remember, liquidated damages affect the allocation of risk and, thus, may impact such issues as pricing, competition, and the cost and difficulty of contract administration.

The assessment of fixed liquidated damages is subject to some limitations. The most important of these is that the fixed amount must be reasonable. Reasonableness is determined by situation; but, where liquidated damages are construed to be a penalty, the clause is not enforceable. The use of boilerplate liquidated damages provisions is not a good idea. The reasonableness criterion demands a best effort estimate on a case-by-case basis. Many organizations routinely set fixed liquidated damages unreasonably low. In cases when the public agency sets a fixed cost for liquidated damages, if delays cost more money than the fixed liquidated damage amount, the public agency is not entitled to recover actual damages.

There are also a number of conditions that entitle the contractor to relief from assessment of liquidated damages. An excusable delay is such a condition. Where an excusable delay exists, the public agency can accelerate performance to achieve the initial delivery or completion target, but that would require an equitable adjustment. An example of a clause for liquidated damages for construction is contained in FAR 52.212-5, which reads as follows:

> (a) If the Contractor fails to complete the work within the time specified in the contract, or any extension, the Contractor shall pay the Government as liquidated damages, the sum of (insert amount) for each day of delay.
> (b) If the Government terminates the Contractor's right to proceed, the resulting damage will consist of liquidated damages until such reasonable time as may be required for final completion of the work together with any increased costs occasioned the Government in completing the work.
> (c) If the Government does not terminate the Contractor's right to proceed, the resulting damage will consist of liquidated damages until the work is completed or accepted.

References

Cibinic, J., Jr., & Nash, R. C., Jr. (1995). *Administration of government contracts* (3rd ed.). Washington, DC: The George Washington University.

Federal Acquisition Regulations Web Site, www.arnet.gov/far/loadmainre.html.

Harney, D. (1992). *Service contracting—A local government guide*. Washington, DC: International City/County Management Association (ICMA)

Smith, L. Y., & Roberson, G. G. (1977). Business law uniform commercial code (4th ed.). Saint Paul, MN: West Publishing.

Thai, Ph.D., K.V. (NIGP 2007). *Introduction to public procurement. (2rd ed.).* Herndon, VA: NIGP.

Chapter 14

Contract Closeout Activities

C ontract closeout is necessary when the work required by the contract is physically complete. Many functions are examined to ensure that the contract terms and conditions have been met, that payments have been properly made, and that other matters, such as satisfactory performance, warranties, technical data requirements, and patents, are documented and closed.

Generally, contract closeout is a formal process for complex procurements, particularly those involving capital projects and extensive service provisions. The time and level of effort to accomplish contract closeout is driven by the complexity and size of the contract. Notwithstanding complexity and size, the Contracting Officer is well advised to utilize a checklist, which includes all matters that must be examined, validated, and officially closed to complete the contract and its records. This chapter will provide the following:

- General guidelines and considerations for contract closeout
- A standard checklist
- A sample of a Contract Closeout Form utilized by the United States National Aeronautics and Space Administration is included as Appendix D.
- The Value of Contract Administration Analysis

General Guidelines

A t or near completion of physical work, contract closeout begins. The contract closeout checklist must be completed prior to closeout to ensure that all required documentation is in the contract files.

After final acceptance and final payment has been made, a Contract Completion Statement should be prepared. Various members of the Contract Administration Team will participate in the closeout process as they provide information that the Contracting Officer or other designated official needs to officially state that the contract is complete in its entirety and may be closed and properly archived.

Closeout files will include a variety of information. For example, general and contract correspondence should be examined to ensure that it is included in the appropriate contract files. Duplicates should be removed. The closeout file must contain the official contract and include all modifications and deliverables received under the contract. If deliverables were voluminous, a letter of transmittal indicating submission of the deliverable (and a letter or other form of acceptance indicating that the government has accepted the deliverable) should be included in the official contract file.

After final acceptance and final payment has been made, a Contract Completion Statement should be prepared.

The contract file must indicate that all reports, deliverables, and other items required under the contract have been received and accepted. Payments made under the contract must be validated to ensure that they have been properly made. Overpayments and underpayments must be reconciled as part of the closeout process.

Performance and progress reports should be included in the contract file. This contract file will serve as the official file within the archives, so the inclusion of all necessary information is vital. At some future time, there may be a need to examine the contract file, and its usefulness is predicated on the extent to which it is reliable and accurate.

As part of the closeout process, the contractor should be required to submit a report of inventions, patents, and copyrights, if such activities or issues could be related directly to, or associated with, the contract. A report affirming that no inventions, patents, or copyrights resulted from the contract would also be proper. In doing so, the Contracting Officer avoids later assertions about inventions, patents, and copyrights that could prove costly and difficult to resolve.

If the contract has provided the contractor with the use of government property, equipment, and/or material, a joint, physical inventory should be conducted as part of the closeout process. The record of the inventory should be included in the contract file.

General Checklist

The following issues should be considered in conjunction with closeout activities.

Administrative Issues

- Is the central contract file complete, and does it conform to regulations governing contract administration as specified by the public agency?
- If the central contract file consists of multiple files, have they been sequentially numbered and identified?
- Does the central file include the file of the Contracting Officer and the Contracting Officer's Representative?
- Did the contract specify a period of performance; and, if yes, has that period of performance ended?
- Have all file documents been signed with original signatures? This would include invoices/vouchers, letters to contractor, memoranda, official correspondence, etc.
- Has the de-obligation of funds been accomplished, if required?
- Have all change orders been defined and included in the central file?
- Have all final determinations been completed?
- Have all optional provisions expired?
- Are there any time extensions pending?
- Have all modification documents been signed?

Deliverables

- Is the final Receiving Report signed and dated?
- Did the Contracting Officer Representative certify that all deliverables have been received and accepted?

Payments and Invoices

- Have all disallowed payments, performance, deliverables, or suspended costs been resolved?

- Has all reconciliation been completed in conjunction with a financial report to verify that all payments have been paid?

- Have any refunds, rebates, and/or credits been annotated in the file?

- Have all excess funds, such as un-liquidated obligations, been verified and submitted to the Finance Department?

Property

- Has the property inventory been received from the contractor?

- Has there been an accounting of all Government-owned property, real or personal, either furnished by the Government or acquired by the contractor for the account of the Government?

- Has appropriate disposal action been taken upon physical completion of the contract/delivery order?

- Has there been a final disposition of Government-furnished property?

Contract Administration Analysis

The final step in the contract management cycle is to conduct an analysis of the contract administration process. After the contract has been closed out, the documentation compiled during the contract administration phase should be reviewed to determine if any changes in the contract administration process would be beneficial to future contracts. The Contractor and the end-user should complete a contract analysis report card. The following areas of the process should be reviewed:

Contract Development

- Were the contract goals adequate?
- Are there are any changes that could be made in the contract document to better handle the agency's needs such as additional contract clauses or different language?

Contract Administration

- Did the contract administration team require additional training?
- Did any unanticipated problems occur?
- What could be done differently or better?

Incorporating these changes into the next contract management cycle and updating the general contract types and clauses is an important final step of contract administration.

Recommended Readings

American Bar Association (2001). *The 2000 Model Procurement Code for State and Local Governments.* Washington, DC: American Bar Association.

Cibinic, J. R., & Nash, C. R., Jr. (1998). *Administration of government contracts.* Washington, DC: George Washington University Press.

DelDuca, L. F. (1996). *Annotations to the Model Procurement Code for state and local governments* (3rd ed.). Washington, DC: American Bar Association.

Engelbeck, M. (2002). *Acquisition management.* Vienna, VA: Management Concepts, Inc.

Gordon, S. B. (1993). *Purchasing for institutions and governmental organizations* (5th ed.). New York: McGraw-Hill, Inc.

McKenna, Conner & Cuneo (1983). *Government contract seminar workbook.* Newbury Park, CA: Sage.

Meiners, A. C. (1995). *Fundamentals of the acquisition process.* Acton, MA: Copley Publishing Group.

Nash, R. C. (Professor Emeritus), O'Brien, K., & Schooner, S. (1998). *The government contracts reference book: A comprehensive guide to the language of procurement* (2nd ed.). Washington, DC: The George Washington University Press.

National Association of State Procurement Officials (NASPO) (2001). *State and local government purchasing principles and practices.* Lexington, KY: NASPO.

Sherman, N. S. (1985, 1991, 1999). *Government procurement management.* Germantown, MD: Woodcrafters Publications.

Appendix A

Sample Conflict Of Interest Form

Acknowledgement of Review Of Ethical Practices
and Conflict of Interest Statutes and Policies

I have been assigned/requested to participate in the following project/task/duty related to the acquisition of goods, services and utilities by the (Agency).

(Insert paragraph describing project/task/duty and potential responders, contractors or vendors, if possible.)

_____ I certify that I do not have any conflicts of interest with this project/task/duty in accordance with (Agency) statute _____. I am aware of my personal responsibility to prevent myself, the (Department) and (Agency) from being placed in a situation where a conflict of interest might exist or could give the appearance of existing.

_____ I further certify that, if I am a manager or a supervisor, it is my personal responsibility to assist staff who work for or with me from placing themselves, the (Department) and the (Agency) in a situation where a conflict of interest might exist or could give the appearance of existing.

_____ I certify that I have read and understand the requirements of the (Agency's) Data Practices Act as they relate to my duties and activities related to the acquisition of goods, services and utilities and will act accordingly.

_____ I have a potential conflict of interest or a situation in which there might be the appearance of a conflict of interest and will be unable to perform the project/task/duties as described. I have informed the project manager of this situation.

Signed: _____   Date: _____

Sample Conflict of Interest Form.

Appendix B

Sample Contract Provision for Restricted Rights Software

Commercial Computer Software—Restricted Rights (June 1987)

(a) As used in this clause, "restricted computer software" means any computer program, computer data base, or documentation thereof, that has been developed at private expense and either is a trade secret, is commercial or financial and confidential or privileged, or is published and copyrighted.

(b) Notwithstanding any provisions to the contrary contained in any Contractor's standard commercial license or lease agreement pertaining to any restricted computer software delivered under this purchase order/contract, and irrespective of whether any such agreement has been proposed prior to or after issuance of this purchase order/contract or of the fact that such agreement may be affixed to or accompany the restricted computer software upon delivery, vendor agrees that the Government shall have the rights that are set forth in paragraph (c) of this clause to use, duplicate or disclose any restricted computer software delivered under this purchase order/contract. The terms and provisions of this contract, including any commercial lease or license agreement, shall be subject to paragraph (c) of this clause and shall comply with Federal laws and the Federal Acquisition Regulation.

(c)(1) The restricted computer software delivered under this contract may not be used, reproduced or disclosed by the Government except as provided in paragraph (c)(2) of this clause or as expressly stated otherwise in this contract.

(2) The restricted computer software may be—

(i) Used or copied for use in or with the computer or computers for which it was acquired, including use at any Government installation to which such computer or computers may be transferred;

(ii) Used or copied for use in or with backup computer if any computer for which it was acquired is inoperative;

(iii) Reproduced for safekeeping (archives) or backup purposes;

(iv) Modified, adapted, or combined with other computer software, provided that the modified, combined, or adapted portions of the derivative software incorporating any of the delivered, restricted computer software shall be subject to same restrictions set forth in this purchase order/contract;

(v) Disclosed to and reproduced for use by support service Contractors or their subcontractors, subject to the same restrictions set forth in this purchase order/contract; and

(vi) Used or copied for use in or transferred to a replacement computer.

(3) If the restricted computer software delivered under this purchase order/ contract is published and copyrighted, it is licensed to the Government, without disclosure prohibitions, with the rights set forth in paragraph (c) (2) of this clause unless expressly stated otherwise in this purchase order/ contract.

(4) To the extent feasible the Contractor shall affix a Notice substantially as follows to any restricted computer software delivered under this purchase order/contract; or, if the vendor does not, the Government has the right to do so:

Notice—Notwithstanding any other lease or license agreement that may pertain to, or accompany the delivery of, this computer software, the rights of the Government regarding its use, reproduction and disclosure are as set forth in Government Contract (or Purchase Order) No. _____.

(d) If any restricted computer software is delivered under this contract with the copyright notice of 17 U.S.C. 401, it will be presumed to be published and copyrighted and licensed to the Government in accordance with paragraph (c) (3) of this clause, unless a statement substantially as follows accompanies such copyright notice:

Unpublished—rights reserved under the copyright laws of the United States.

(END OF CLAUSE)

Appendix C

Excerpt from NASA's Handbook on Contract Data

99-20

Procurement Information Circular

November 10, 1999

CONTRACTOR-GENERATED DATA

PURPOSE: To assure that necessary contractor-generated data are obtained contractually, and that unnecessary data are not.

PROBLEM: NASA managers are not obtaining all of the contractor-generated data they need to perform their duties with respect to the management of NASA projects and programs, maintaining official records, and reporting to other Public Agency offices. Examples include:

1. The software Independent Verification and Validation (IV&V) Facility reported difficulty in obtaining software discrepancy data (e.g., problem reports, discrepancy reports, defect databases, anomalies, errors, faults) from contractors relative to program software development activities. This information is necessary in order to predict software latency rates, assess software test/method/practice effectiveness, and quantify Return On Investment (ROI) for software IV&V.

2. In recent years only half of the known facilities maintenance expenses were reflected in the NASA Financial and Contractual Status system. This problem has occurred in aerospace projects where facilities maintenance related expense is incidental relative to the overall cost of the project, and the contract does not require the explicit breakout of facilities maintenance data as part of the cost reporting requirement. The cumulative omission of that data is significant, and has necessitated a manual collection of the data. Manual collection is unnecessarily time consuming, and often arrives too late for inclusion in the budget cycle.

3. The resource management community has reported difficulty in obtaining contractor FTE data. Contractor FTE data is essential to support safety planning, as well as reporting requirements to the Office of Management and Budget, and to NASA internal offices, e.g., the Independent Annual Review teams, Program Management Council, and Institutional Program Offices.

Conversely, if there is no critical review of the planned contract data requirements with respect to the bona fide need to acquire the data, the Public Agency risks incurring expenses that are substantial and unnecessary.

BACKGROUND: NASA needs to obtain data related to the performance of its contracts, e.g., to monitor contractor performance, to develop historical data for estimating the cost of follow-on work, to support budget requests, etc. Before Performance-based Contracting (PBC) became common, it was customary to obtain necessary data from the contractors informally. That is, when a need for data was identified that was not already covered under the contract data requirements list (CDRL), the contractor was simply requested to furnish the data. Under level-of-effort, cost reimbursement contracts, that simple arrangement was convenient and acceptable to both parties. However, under PBC, contractors tend, quite justifiably, to resist requests for effort not explicitly required by the contract because that effort will increase their baseline costs. It is necessary to do better advance planning when preparing to award a contract in order to make sure that all data needs are identified at the outset. The project/program office uses some of that data, and other data are used by functional or other organizations, such as the data that flows into the NASA Financial Management System from contractor NF 533 submissions. Therefore, it is important that all stakeholders have the opportunity to obtain the data that they need. Moreover, the Associate Administrator for Procurement is responsible for ensuring that contracts require contractors to provide functional management costs to be used in the NASA accounting system. These principles are already required by NASA policy referenced below.

Furthermore, when buying data, bear in mind that the purpose of a statement of work (SOW) is to describe the contractor's work, including a description of that work necessary to generate contract-required data. A Data Requirements Document (DRD) or Data Item Description (DID) should be used to describe the format and content of the data product(s) to be generated; and the CDRL should be used to describe the Public Agency's delivery instructions for the data.

Finally, contracting officers are reminded that the requirement for contractors to deliver data is material to contract performance. If data are not submitted as required by the contract, then the contracting officer should consider exercising appropriate contractual remedies.

SUMMARY: Contracting Officers must ensure that all stakeholders (financial management office, safety office, IV and V Facility, et al.) have had the opportunity to identify their needs for data. Specific data requirements documents may need to be developed/tailored to meet specific data requirements, and included in the contract as "deliverables." Please ensure that Center procedures provide for pre-contract data requirements review, and that that review considers both the inclusion of necessary data requirements and the exclusion of unnecessary data requirements.

POLICY REFERENCES: NPD 9501.1F, NASA Contractor Financial Management Reporting System; NPG 9501.2C, NASA Contractor Financial Management Reporting; NPD 8831.1B, Management of Facilities Maintenance; and NPD 2820.1, NASA Software Policies.

Appendix D

Sample of NASA's Contract Closeout Checklist

National Aeronautics and Space Administration Contract Closeout Checklist				
1. Name of Contractor	**2. Contract Number**	**3. Contract Amendment (Modifications Numbered Through)**		**4. Physical - Completion Date**
Action Items		**Forecast For Completion**	**Action Initiated**	**Action Completed**
Initial Funds Review Completed				
Excess Funds Deobligated (If Applicable)				
Quick Closeout Procedures Considered				
Disposition of Classified Material Completed				
Final New Technology Report Submitted (Inventions Disclosure)				
Final Patent Rights Report Cleared (NASA Form 1626)				
Settlement of All Interim or Disallowed Costs (NASA Form 456)				
Final Royalty Report Cleared				
Plant Clearance Report Received (DD Form 1593)				
Property Clearance Received (NASA Form 1018)				
Settlement of All Interim or Disallowed Costs (NASA Form 456)				
Price Revision Completed				
Settlement of Subcontracts by The Prime Contractor Completed				

Prior Year Overhead Rates Completed			
Contractor's Closing Statement Received			
Termination Docket Completed (NASA Form 1413)			
Contract Audit Completed			
Contractor Assignment and Release (NASA Form 778)			
Final Voucher Submitted			
Final Paid Voucher Received			
Final Removal of Excess Funds Recommended			
Assignee's Assignment of Refunds, Rebates, Credits, and Other Amounts (NASA Form 781)			
Contractor's Assignment of Refunds, Rebates, Credits, and Other Amounts (NASA Form 780)			
Disposition of Outstanding Value Engineering Change Proposals (If Applicable)			
Issuance of Contract Completion Statement (NASA Form 1611)			
Other Requirements Completed (Specify)			
Typed Name and Title of Responsible official			
SIGNATURE OF RESPONSIBLE OFFICIAL (Sign only upon completion of all actions)			DATE
NASA Form 1612		MAR 93 Previous Edition is Obsolete	Computer-Generated

Index

About the Authors

 Elisabeth Wright is a member of the full time faculty of the School of International Graduate Studies at the US Naval Postgraduate School in Monterey, CA. She is also the Program Manager for the International Defense Acquisition Resources Management program at the school. Prior to her appointment, she served on the faculty of the University of Mary Washington and as the Director of the Master of Science Program in Acquisition Management at the George Washington University, School of Business and Public Management. Professor Wright holds her doctorate from the University of Southern California, School of Policy, Planning and Development and additional degrees from Florida Tech and the University of Maryland. Prior to her career in academia, she was a senior level acquisition manager within the Department of the Navy and the Department of Energy. Professor Wright is designated a Certified Professional Contracts Manager (CPCM) and was awarded the distinction of Fellow by the National Contract Management Association. She has authored numerous articles on procurement and contracting and is an internationally recognized expert in the field.

 William D. Davison, CPPO, is the Director of Purchasing for Stearns County, MN. He is responsible for the purchase of all goods, services and construction for the county, including the mail center, central receiving and the copy center. Prior to that, he was the Director of Purchasing for the College of St. Catherine.

Mr. Davison holds a Master of Science in Procurement and Contract Administration from Florida Tech and a Bachelor of Science in Economics from the University of Minnesota. Mr. Davison was the Project Manager for the NIGP 2000 Contract Management text. In 2000, Mr. Davison was named by NIGP as the National Manager of the Year. He has had several research papers on contract administration accepted for publication and is an internationally recognized expert in the fields of procurement and contract management.

Other books published by the
National Institute of Governmental Purchasing, Inc. (NIGP):

INTRODUCTION TO PUBLIC PROCUREMENT

THE LEGAL ASPECTS OF PUBLIC PURCHASING

DEVELOPING AND MANAGING REQUESTS FOR PROPOSALS IN THE PUBLIC SECTOR

SOURCING IN THE PUBLIC SECTOR

STRATEGIC PROCUREMENT PLANNING IN THE PUBLIC SECTOR

FUNDAMENTALS OF LEADERSHIP AND MANAGEMENT IN PUBLIC PROCUREMENT

ALTERNATIVE DISPUTE RESOLUTION

CONTRACTING FOR PUBLIC SECTOR SERVICES

CAPITAL ACQUISITIONS

LOGISTICS AND TRANSPORTATION

RISK MANAGEMENT IN PUBLIC CONTRACTING

WAREHOUSING AND INVENTORY CONTROL

CONTRACTING FOR CONSTRUCTION SERVICES